Andrew Watts

Façades
Technical Review

RIBA Publishing

Publishing partners

Paroc Panel System UK Ltd designs and manufactures stone wool fire proof composite panel systems for commercial and industrial applications, including cladding panels, interior partition walls and interior ceilings. In addition to the standard systems, the range includes acoustic and thermal insulation panel systems, and a fireproof panel solution. All systems are available in a wide standard and specialist colours and finishes for internal or external cladding applications.

Denis Beardmore
Paroc Panel System UK Ltd
Stoney Lane
Rainhill
Prescot
Merseyside
L35 9LL

Tel: 0151 426 6555
Fax: 0151 426 6622

denis.beardmore@paroc.com
www.paroc.com

weber building solutions is an international manufacturer of building mortars with factories throughout Europe, the Far East and South America. In the UK and Ireland, weber has grown from the amalgamation of four well known and respected bands; Eglinton, Howtex, SBD and Snowcem. The company has developed an unparalleled depth of knowledge and experience in the fields of External Wall Insulation, Tile fixing, Technical Mortars, Concrete Repair, and Renders and Finishes. The first company to develop external wall insulation systems in the UK and the pioneer of Monocouche renders worldwide, weber offers a valuable resource to specifiers who wish to develop façades that both look good and perform.

weber building solutions
Dickens House
Enterprise Way
Maulden Road
Flitwick
Bedfordshire
MK45 5BY

Tel: 08703 330070
Fax: 01525 718988

mail@weberbuildingsolutions.co.uk
www.weberbuildingsolutions.co.uk

contents

This Façades Technical Review is the first in a series of books from RIBA Publishing which aims to show what is current in the technical aspects of building design. Façade design has become increasingly specialised in recent years as the technology is developed, in part from outside the traditions of building construction. The need for repetition of components, which has long been one of the main principles of manufacturing and of 20th Century design, is no longer a primary guiding principle, as components can increasingly be developed economically for a single building project. The renewed interest in the craft of façade construction, of making parts of a building envelope as mock-ups and prototypes in workshops and design studios is set to further the interest in bringing the details of façades to new levels of innovation.

Most façade design is still based on working with a particular material or generic system based on a particular material. Working with a building material involves understanding its essential nature – its physical properties that give rise to certain possibilities for use which can lead to a quite unexpected appearance during the design development. The character of the material can also be a starting point – the visual qualities of battered road vehicles, transport containers or of plywood signboards for example. While the source material, such as transport containers, are not designed for long term use, they sometimes serve as a starting point for the development of a façade system, where building designs, especially façades and roofs, are being generated from sources outside the traditional vocabulary of architecture.

This technical review discusses façade systems in terms of the primary material used: metal, glass, concrete, masonry, plastics and timber, in order of decreasing density from

Pavilion, Son en Breugel, Belgium. Architect: NOX/Lars Spuybroek

H2O Café, Graz, Austria. Architect: Acconci Studio

H2O Café, Graz, Austria. Architect: Acconci Studio

The use of monocoque construction is being gradually developed in building projects. The Winery House Project by Marcello Spina+Guillermo Banchini is an aluminium framed design that uses metal sheet as a stressed skin to provide a continuity of flowing surfaces that are far removed from the language of traditional timber framing. The H_2O Café in Graz by Acconci Studio uses a shell structure clad in a series of opaque and translucent panels to create semi-enclosed circulation spaces and a fully enclosed café. The Pavilion at Son en Breugel, Belgium by NOX/Lars Spuybroek is a more sculptural development of the shell concept in a mixture of metal framing and mesh.

Winery House Project, Sydney, Australia. Architect: Patterns/Marcello Spina+Guillermo Banchini

Maison Folie, Lille-Wazemmes, France. Architect: NOX

Winery House Project, Sydney, Australia. Architect: Patterns/Marcello Spina+Guillermo Banchini

heavyweight to lightweight. With each material the most common generic methods are discussed. Each generic system is reviewed in terms of the primary design considerations, which are mainly its appearance resulting from different methods of fixing or of material size. The design solutions, mainly at junctions resulting from the different ways of applying these systems, and working with the primary material, are then set out, with an emphasis on current applications in contemporary design. The details shown are generic as a general setting-out of the principles of assembly rather than as individual case studies of specific buildings which would have little general application and from which it would be difficult to find more general applications for their use in façade design. Under the heading of Design Considerations, systems and their essential assembly are discussed in order to suggest how it might be manipulated or adapted for a specific design. The following section on Design Solutions focuses on

interfaces and how systems are applied as standard solutions. Examining one technique may suggest to the reader its use in a different material or for a different purpose. This Technical Review is aimed to be fuel for ideas and development in façade design.

The relationship between appearance and technique, between aesthetics and technology, should be viewed by the reader both forwards and backwards, and not necessarily as a simple narrative of requirements and solutions, from visual idea to detail, and from detail back to the primary material used. This interaction of the complete design process through many iterations is of course an essential part of architectural design, from sketch concept through to design development and prototyping which in turn informs the design concept. This completely interactive process of design development would have been difficult to implement even 10 years ago. In terms of examples chosen, buildings not specifically from the UK are illustrated to widen aware-

ness and interest in examples from around the world in different cultures and conditions of building construction.

Developments in façade systems

In terms of materials used, designers have long been fascinated by representations of architectural ideas in drawn and model form and seeing possibilities for the imagery created to be used directly in buildings – the built 'model' rather than the re-interpretation of an architectural idea using conventional construction techniques. Much of technical development of façade designs is in trying to ensure that as much of the energy of the design process finds its way into finished building as a dynamic process.

The development of 'structural envelopes' in glazed façades has evolved over the past 15 years from concepts based on the fuselages of aircraft to full loadbearing structures for glazed walls. This method involves the development of curtain walling from cladding

3

Mobile architecture and the idea of building as operable machines is finding expression in mobile working studios formed as lightweight building envelopes. The Studio at Utrecht by Korteknie Stuhlmacher uses timber framed panels which can be lowered to form deck space. The Cocobello by Peter Haimerl unfolds from a compact, transportable shape and deploys itself to form larger spaces within. Its envelope uses a metal frame clad in metal panels.

Mobile Artist's Studio in Utrecht. Architect: Korteknie Stuhlmacher Architecten

Mobile Artist's Studio in Utrecht. Architect: Korteknie Stuhlmacher Architecten

Cocobello. Mobile Studio. Architect: Peter Haimerl

to a full loadbearing wall. Aluminium or small section steel frames are replaced by larger sections that can support the edges of structural floor slabs rather than being supported by them. This allows columns to be omitted from the edges of floors, giving a glazed wall a visual quality that is quite different from that seen next to a wall framed by structural columns. The idea has been developed for use in both flat and curved façades where only a trapezoidal-shaped metal frame is visible. This technique has been applied successfully on large-scale buildings with stick and unitised glazing using both pressure plate and silicone bonded techniques.

The increased reliability of metal cladding systems has led to their use as a source of visual texture rather than as primarily economic cladding systems. The ability of the metals to provide characteristic patina has long been used on roofs but this is now appearing in façades, with even the use of weathering steel for both external wall panels

and window frames. The greater reliability of long term performance of waterproof membranes for metal rainscreens and folded seam metal façades has led to increasingly ambitious uses of the material where the metal can take on forms that are not obliged to follow the principles of traditional façade construction. Folded metal panels are using more textured finishes and rainscreens with complex geometries, sometimes with cut-outs and contours that explore the deeper possibilities of this construction method. The use of stainless steel mesh and perforated sheet have developed from flat, taut skins to 3D forms with a high degree of modelling. The translucent, lightweight qualities of mesh and punched sheet are being achieved without a visually heavy supporting structure that previously hindered interest in these materials.

A development in concrete construction, parallel to the use of self-supporting walls in glazing, is of the orthogonal arrangement of concrete walls and window openings has

given way to non-linear geometry in new projects. This has a parallel in GRC (glass fibre reinforced concrete) where the material is being moulded in more complex textures that are non-repetitive. This is partly due to the use of synthetic rubber mats in moulds which can now be made relatively economically. The surface texture of GRC can take on a smooth, continuous appearance that is free of board marks and formwork joints associated with in situ cast concrete, even on façades where a move away from a rectilinear grid of window openings has been taken.

A major development in masonry has been the use of very thin renders on thermal insulation set on the outside of blockwork-based walls. They provide a traditional looking finish that is part of a highly insulated wall that is also able to use its thermal mass. Where brick and blockwork are visible on the outside, there is also a tendency to increasingly abstract its appearance away from the traditional language of wall and opening, to a series of highly

Wood Deck house, Kamarura, Japan. Architect: Tezuka Architects

Shopping Centre, Lisbon, Portugal. Architect: Promontorio

The examples on this page are buildings with varied façade textures within a single, simply defined building form. The box-like form of the Wood Deck House by Tezuka Architects has timber cladding on a steel framed box-like structure which allows different systems to be applied to a single façade from a single material.

The Dutch Embassy in Berlin by OMA uses a unitised glazing system to provide a varied façade from a single system within a relatively simple external building form. The Ecoms House by Riken Yamamoto and Field Shop uses honeycomb framed aluminium panels which are bolted together to form a loadbearing wall that supports floor decks and roof made from extruded aluminium panels as part of a complete building system. The Shopping Centre in Lisbon by Promentorio has a simple building enclosure formed in profiled metal sheet which is painted to provide a varied façade resulting from the graphic.

Ecoms House, Tosu-City, Saga, Japan. Architect: Riken Yamamoto and Field Shop

Dutch Embassy, Berlin, Germany. Architect: Office for Metropolitan Architecture

5

geometric solids and voids that do not reveal the nature of the support system behind. This reflects the fact that the masonry walls are rarely loadbearing but are often a cladding material supported on a metal carrier system. Rather than use these systems to imitate the traditional visual forms of the material, brick and blockwork explore the possibilities of these stainless steel fixing systems and what they can achieve in their own terms. In some cases this leads to an imitation of the language of other materials – that of reinforced concrete for example, where cut-outs can be formed without the need to introduce separate beams and supporting structure.

Developments in the use of plastics in façades are not limited to single materials such as polycarbonate and GRP but are used in composite materials with materials such as plywood sheet and polymer-based fabrics. Visually lightweight external walls, both loadbearing and as cladding elements have been developed for individual houses, as extensions to existing buildings and as roof structures. GRP laid onto plywood as a waterproofing layer to a timber framed structure is a development of ideas developed in the 1960s, while the use of polymer foams clad in a single layer membrane gives highly insulated and waterproof enclosures to forms

that would otherwise be realised only in reinforced concrete, with the high costs and difficulties in waterproofing and insulating such sculptural forms in that material. The possibilities of highly insulated, highly sculptural forms in this economic, yet durable material are finding greater appreciation.

The use of timber framing and cladding for buildings has gained considerable popularity over the past 15 years as concerns about the environmental impact of building materials has outweighed the traditional concerns of timber as an easily combustible building material. The more ambitious use of timber frames, in developing a wide range of forms

Thick wall assembly. Scale 1:25.

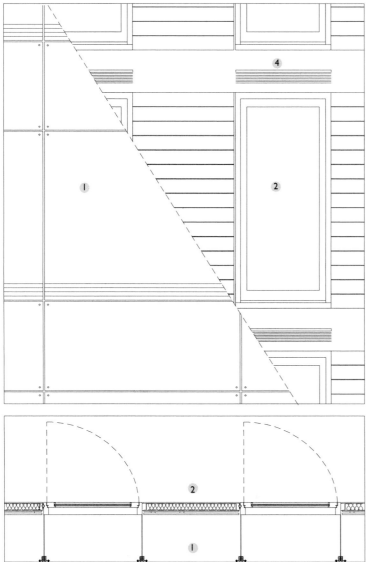

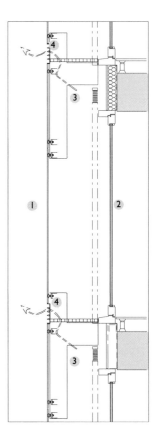

A thin wall with an outer sealed single glazed skin of framed glazing. An inner skin of double glazed doors provides maintenance access to a cavity containing retractable blinds. The heat build-up from solar radiation in the void is extracted by mechanical ventilation in the void above the blinds, adjacent to the floor zone. The warmed air is used by the building's mechanical ventilation system.

1.   Outer skin of framed glazing, sealed.
2.   Inner skin of aluminium framed doors.
3.   Retractable blinds.
4.   Zone for air extraction.

Thin wall assembly. Scale 1:25.

A thin wall with an outer sealed single glazed skin of framed glazing. An inner skin of double glazed doors provides maintenance access to a cavity containing retractable blinds. The heat build-up from solar radiation in the void is extracted by mechanical ventilation in the void above the blinds, adjacent to the floor zone. The warmed air is used by the building's mechanical ventilation system.

1. Outer skin of framed glazing, sealed.
2. Inner skin of aluminium framed doors.
3. Retractable blinds.
4. Zone for air extraction to mechanical ventilation.

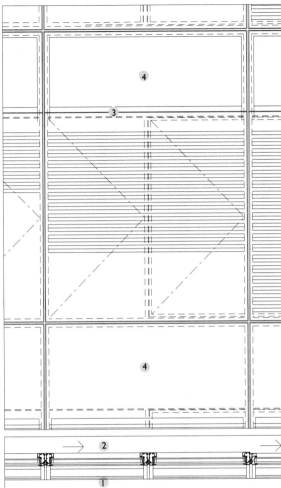

from outside those of traditional construction, from amphibious vehicles to transport containers and hangars, has given an enormous boost to the use of the material. These developments allow the lightweight nature of timber to be exploited, with folding shutters and lifting panels being incorporated into envelopes that when closed look like a homogenous timber box and when opened along visually hairline joints, create a highly modelled façade, linked to open balconies and large scale windows that are not usually associated with timber construction. This toolbox-like approach to the form of façades is set to develop in all façade construction materials over the next 10 years.

Twin wall façades

An important development in façade design has been in the introduction of 'twin wall' or 'double wall' façades as a method of providing natural ventilation, increasing daylighting and promoting the use of thermal mass for

night time cooling in buildings, which can provide substantial energy savings in mechanical ventilation. These façades still have relatively few moving parts (which would make them more flexible in their use) due to the additional costs involved. Fixed shading systems, are considerably cheaper than those with moveable screens or louvres, but they cannot move in response to the path of the sun, or to changing weather conditions and different times of year. In double wall façades the solar shading is installed in the void between inner and outer skins, where the blinds are better protected and where they are more effective. Conventional single layer glazed walls attempt to resolve conflicting performance requirements within a single layer. Solar control layers in glass have the effect of reducing the transparency of external walls, which increases the amount of electrical lighting required internally. Layered façades separate out functions of waterproofing, solar control and ventilation in different configurations. In

twin wall façades these have become two generic types: thick walls and thin walls.

In thick twin walls, an outer layer, typically a single skin of glass is separated from an inner wall by a ventilated cavity of between 750mm and 1000mm. The inner skin typically comprises a double glazed curtain wall with opening windows. Because the outer wall is protecting the inner wall from windblown rain, materials other than metal and glass can be used to form the inner wall, such as timber and polycarbonate sheet. Air is passed through the outer wall into the zone between the two skins. This is done either with open jointed, or partially open joints in the outer glazed wall, or alternatively with openable controls at floor level which admit air at different times of day and at different times of the year. The second method provides a method of closely controlling cavity ventilation, but is considerably more expensive to install. Both methods are used in taller buildings where the wind speed is often too high to allow windows to

Matsunoyama Natural Science Museum, Japan. Architect: Tezuka Architects

Control Post, Middelburg, Holland. Architect: BAR Architects

Reflex HQ, Treviso. Italy. Architect: Cesare Monti-Gemini Studio

be opened safely. Walkways are set into the void, usually at floor levels, to allow the glass surfaces facing into the void to be cleaned and maintained easily. Depending on the height of the façade, the natural ventilation provided by this configuration uses external wind pressure to provide fresh air into the void as well as the stack effect to allow the heat gained within the void, in warm weather, to escape to the outside. The outer skin also provides solar shading, and can absorb solar energy. In winter, where solar gain is a much less significant issue, the open jointed outer skin can suffer from cold air being allowed to enter the void, but the void can also act as a winter buffer zone. The method of using metal flaps and louvres allows the quantity and frequency of fresh air entering the void to be more closely controlled.

Thin wall façades comprise two skins of glass set closely together, with a cavity in the region of 100mm wide. The cavity is mechanically ventilated, allowing it to be considerably smaller in depth than the naturally ventilated thick wall design. Air can be drawn up through the cavity from outside or from inside, the air drawn through the façade being separate from the mechanical ventilation for the building. The inner skin has a series of opening doors to allow access into the cavity for cleaning and maintenance. Blinds are usually set into the void in order to provide solar shading. Solar energy absorbed by the blinds is radiated into the cavity where it is drawn away by air rising in the cavity. The warmed air is then ejected at the top of the panel. In winter, warm air extracted from the inside of the building is drawn through into the façade at floor level or in the void below floor level and is drawn up through the external wall to reduce the amount of heat loss through it. When the air into the cavity is provided from inside, the façade is completely sealed, and requires only occasional access to the void for cleaning and maintenance. Façades which are open on the outside require cleaning from the dust drawn into the cavity between the two glass skins.

The Prada Store in Tokyo is constructed as a supporting steel frame to which an aluminium carrier system is fixed directly. Curved double glazed units are mechanically fixed on clips set into a continuous groove formed around the edge of the double glazed units. The gap between the panels is filled with silicone.

The Library in Seattle by OMA uses a capped system which, like the Prada Building, is set onto a metal frame and is secured with pressure plates. This provides a continuous façade texture across a complex building form.

Library, Seattle, USA. Architect: Office for Metropolitan Architecture

The three examples on the opposite page show façades formed from a single primary material. The Natural Science Museum by Tezuka Architects is formed from a continuous skin of welded Corten steel sheet which is also used for the window frames in order to not detract from the continuity of the metal cladding. The Control Post by BAR is a twin wall façade of steel framed panels with fixed lights set behind an outer skin of bolt fixed glazing that forms a complete envelope. The Reflex HQ by Monti-Gemini is a single skin glazed volume that forms a glass box projecting forward of its adjacent opaque façades. The supporting structure of steel rods and castings become visible from outside at night.

Prada Store, Tokyo, Japan. Architect: Herzog+deMeuron

Prada Store, Tokyo, Japan. Architect: Herzog+deMeuron

A recent development in metal façades has been in the use of structural metal panels as a departure from cladding towards loadbearing construction, as illustrated by Riken Yamamoto's Ecoms House. While paint-based finishes are ever-improving in their resistance to colour fading and in their durability, coatings still conceal the 'natural' appearance of the material. A revival in the use of patenated finishes, resulting from the natural (or factory accelerated) weathering of metal surfaces, allows the base material to be seen, as at the Natural Science Museum by Tezuka. Galvanising techniques have also made the use of this zinc – based coating on steel a much more visually consistent finish in its own right, as at the Shopping Centre by Promentorio, particularly when mixed with an applied graphic. The possibilities of metal rainscreen panels to be detached geometrically from their waterproofed backing wall is lending itself to ever more complex forms that exploit the possibilities of this method, as seen in the Langenlois Vineyard by Steven Holl.

01_
metal

Photographs. Top (left to right): Vineyard, Langenlois, Austria. Architect: Steven Holl; Matsunoyama Natural Science Museum, Japan. Architect: Tezuka Architects; Ecoms House, Tosu-City, Saga, Japan. Architect: Riken Yamamoto and Field Shop; Shopping Centre, Lisbon. Architect: Promontorio. Opposite page: Factory, Geneva. Architect: Bernard Tschumi and Associates

Porous/Release, Tagajo Miyagi, Japan. Architect: Naoto Yiegashi+Norm null OFFice

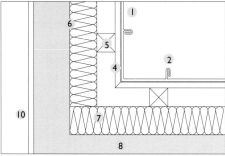

Plan 1:10. Internal corner

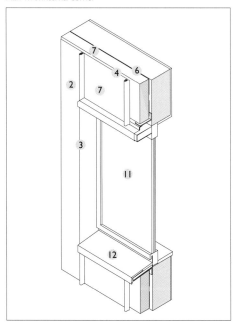

Standing seam wall assembly

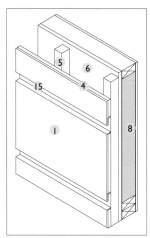

Recessed joint wall assembly

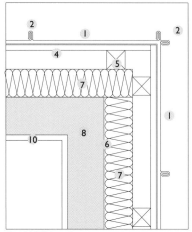

Plan 1:10. External corner

Details

1. Folded metal sheet
2. Standing seam joints
3. Metal flashing
4. Timber-based substrate
5. Fixing battens
6. Waterproof membrane
7. Closed cell thermal insulation
8. Backing wall
9. Roof membrane
10. Internal finish
11. Window frame
12. Folded metal cill
13. Folded metal coping
14. Ventilated metal drip
15. Recessed joint

For both standing seam joints and shingled tiles, openings and edge flashings, including parapets, are formed with folded metal flashings in the same material. Flashings can be set below the material at junctions which reduces their visibility, enhancing the texture of the façade material where required.

The use of shingled tiles has been developed further to provide economic metal façades by using panels of different sizes, and with folded or welded joints, as shown in the photograph.

The use of recessed joints in metal façades has been revived with the use of metal sheets with folded edges that fit into grooves formed in a timber substrate.

Design considerations

Sheet metal that is continuously supported on a substrate provides a system which can closely follow a complex geometry with relative ease, making it very suitable as a covering to a highly modelled façade. This method has developed from its traditional use in roofing, where the standing seam technique is well established. Sheet metal provides an economic outer covering in projects where wall and roof are combined in a single form, or where the external envelope is highly modelled in a single form where one material is required for the complete envelope. The principles of rainwater exclusion used on roofs can be applied, with continuous joint lines, to form a complete envelope from a (nominally) flat roof to vertical wall to inverted soffit conditions.

The two generic methods for supporting sheet metal façades that suit different conditions are continuous standing seams and tiled shingles. Standing seams are suited where long, straight or continuous joint lines are required or where the façade has gentle curves which can be picked out by the joint lines. Tiled shingles are suited to complex geometries and smaller scale applications where a high degree of surface modelling is required. Metal sheet can also be laid onto a timber-based substrate as an outer covering to a complex form.

Standing seam roofs have traditionally had a slightly uneven appearance due to the softer, more ductile metals used, mainly lead, zinc and copper. The 'oil canning' effects of this material, which are visible immediately after installation on both façades and roofs,

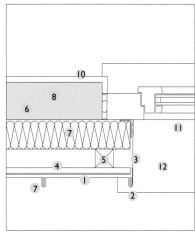

Plan 1:10. Window jamb

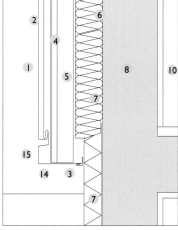

Section 1:10. Ground level cill

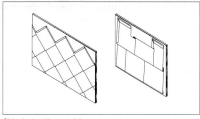

Shingled wall assemblies

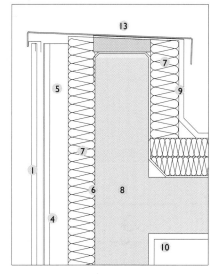

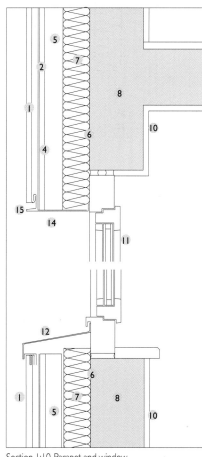

Section 1:10. Parapet and window

tend to diminish as the façade weathers to the characteristic patina of the metal used. The texture remains with weathering, giving a hand crafted appearance which suits visually vibrant façades. Some recent buildings have even slightly exaggerated this effect before installation to create a highly textured surface finish to the metal. Standing seam metal façades have the essential visual characteristic of highly visible joints at relatively close centres of between 450–600mm. This construction method, used traditionally as a roofing system, is used increasingly in façades as an economic system that is easy to combine with other façade elements such as glazing without the need for reveals and visible flashings.

Design solutions

An advantage of continuously supported sheet metal is that the rhythm of standing seams does not need to be coordinated in a modular way with openings in the façade. Flashings can be formed easily at window and door openings and do not require to be aligned with an adjacent standing seam or shingle edge for a reliable joint to be formed. When joints are at close centres, at around 400mm, the joint pattern provides an overall texture for a façade rather than a defining grid. Long lengths of material allow horizontal joints to be avoided in smaller scale applications, up to around 12 metres, but curved or highly modelled façade/roof combinations require closer centres to accommodate the curvature.

Where crisp, straight lines are required in the design, the standing seam method is used on vertical joints, in a variety of configurations,

to suit visual requirements. The choice of seam is primarily visual, ranging from the wide rolled seam of traditional lead roofing to the thin folded projecting seam of traditional zinc and copper roofing. Horizontal joints are often folded to form a flattened seam that allows rainwater to run off it without finding its way into a joint.

Tiled or 'shingled' standing seam metal façades use flattened folded seams on all sides of the panel. Since the same source material of metal strip is used, metal tiles are usually in widths of around 450–600mm depending on the metal used. The jointing system also performs well when the tiles are set diagonally, with 45° being most commonly used in practice.

Both methods use a continuous supporting material, typically plywood sheet for its ability to form complex surfaces with ease. Timber boards are also used, but mainly in open jointed configuration to support zinc sheet, which requires ventilation on its internal face to avoid corrosion. Timber substrates are usually ventilated on their internal face in order to reduce the possibility of damage associated with trapped moisture. An alternative substrate can be formed in rigid thermal insulation, where the metal sheet is mechanically fixed at points to pressed metal rails set into the insulation, which also serve as a continuous support. This method is useful where standing seam metal is used as a waterproofing covering to a concrete wall or masonry wall, where rigid insulation is fixed directly to the backing wall.

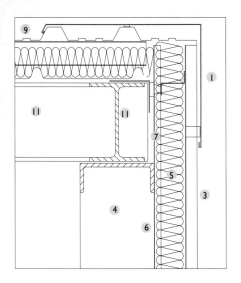

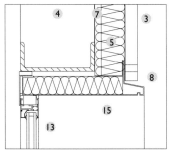

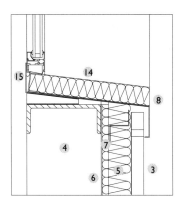

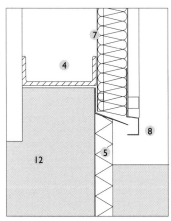

Section 1:10. Parapet, window and ground level

Bombala Farmhouse, New South Wales, Australia. Architect: Collins and Turner

Design considerations

The use of profiled metal cladding has spread from its application in industrial buildings in the 1970's to a more architecturally-based use. This façade system was used primarily as a single material, in either steel or aluminium, for the complete cladding of factory/warehouse type buildings with a large roof area, shallow pitched roofs and a relatively small façade area in relation to that of the roof. The all-metal envelope evolved with the introduction of curved eaves and concealed gutter with walls and roof appearing to be a continuous form. The profiled metal sheet was set with the ribs running from top to bottom of the roof and continued down the façades in the same alignment. As its use in façades developed, profiled metal cladding was used horizontally rather than vertically, and at different angles, as well as with profiles that were intended for roof applications only, such as wide span structural deck systems that gave a very distinctive appearance when used as wall cladding.

The wide range of profiles available, from small wave profiles to deep profiled sections, gives a wide range of visual effects. The main advantage of profiled metal cladding over continuously supported metal is that profiled sheet can span 3–5 metres between supports, depending on the profile used. The profile depth provides rigidity of the material in one direction, allowing it to be fixed to a structural frame rather than requiring the continuous support of a backing wall. Its shape allows the sheet to be curved in one direction during installation on site, with the material lapped on all edges regardless of its orientation. Profiled sheet can be curved along its rigid length by crimping in the factory, usually to form curved corner pieces for horizontally-set cladding, or curved eaves pieces for vertically-set cladding. Proprietary systems offer a range of curved components as well as 90° corners where short lengths of sheet are welded to form a crisp corner panels.

Vertically-set sheeting requires folded metal flashings at the top and bottom of the wall to form parapets and sills, since the flashings are made from flat sheet. Manufacturers provide plastic or foam-based filler pieces to close the gap between the profiled sheet and the flat metal flashings. continuous cladding with barely visible joints resulting from lapping the sheets. Alternatively, horizontally-set sheet can be divided into bays, formed with vertical joints closed with cover strips or with recessed pressed (top hat) sections.

Design solutions

Openings for windows and doors are sealed with metal flashings that can be determined as much by visual requirements as by the needs of weather proofing. Window openings often have wide cover strips around the edges of the opening to provide a full weather tight seal which form a highly visible part of the design.

Corners can be made from either externally set cover strips or by recessed corner flashings to suit the design. The recessed version requires careful installation of the cladding sheets on site in order to achieve the relatively narrow corner joint widths. Cover strips usually have their edge folded back to

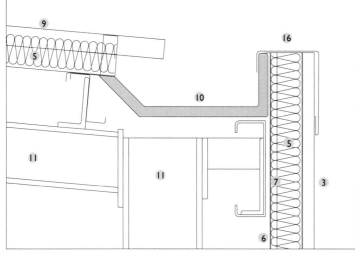

Section 1:10. Parapet

provide a crisp edge.

At roof level, parapets are formed with a pressed metal coping with another flashing beneath. A metal flashing is used to close the gap between the roof deck and the parapet upstand where the roof is also clad in profiled metal sheet. Where only a low upstand is required, as at gables, a folded flashing is fixed to the roof surface to form a sealed edge. A metal coping flashing is then fixed to the upstand and is folded down the face of the external wall. Although the thermal insulation forming part of the wall construction is made continuous with that of the roof, the void in the parapet is usually filled with thermal insulation to avoid high temperature variations between outside and inside the construction.

The void behind the sheet is filled with thermal insulation which requires a vapour barrier on its internal (warm in winter) face. The internal lining of the wall can be in any material, though dry lining or an additional layer of profiled metal sheet is typical. Some manufacturers have proprietary lining sheets in metal which are flatter than the external profiled sheet to suit the typical requirements of internal finishes.

Although proprietary systems are available it is easy to adapt these systems, where the façade fabricator makes flashings to suit individual requirements. Principles of details are well understood by fabricators and complete proprietary systems are not always required.

Details

1. Metal cover strip
2. Horizontally-set profiled sheet
3. Vertically-set profiled sheet
4. Supporting frame / carrier system
5. Thermal insulation
6. Inner lining sheet
7. Vapour barrier
8. Metal drip
9. Roof, profiled metal sheet shown
10. Parapet gutter
11. Supporting structure
12. Structural slab
13. Window frame
14. Pressed metal sill
15. Metal trim to window
16. Metal parapet coping

In the details shown, folded flashings are usually in two layers, with an inner seal between cladding and window, and an additional outer flashing which is sealed with silicone back to the profiled metal.
The example in the photograph shows profiled metal sheet formed into façade bays which are made continuous with the adjacent glazing. Profiled metal sheet is also used to form a complete envelope that provides a strong sense of three dimensional modelling to the building form.

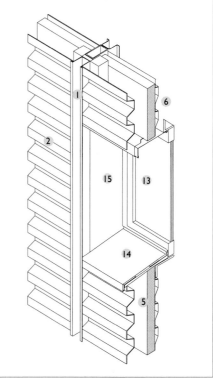

Horizontally-set wall assembly

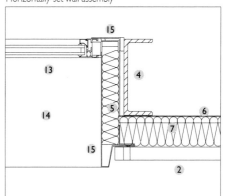

Plan 1:10. Window jamb

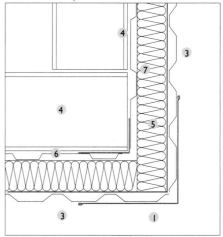

Plan 1:10. External corner

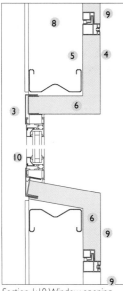

Section 1:10. Window opening

Usera Public Library, Madrid. Architect: Abalos+Herreros

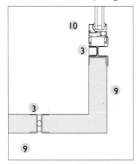

Plan 1:10. Corner with window

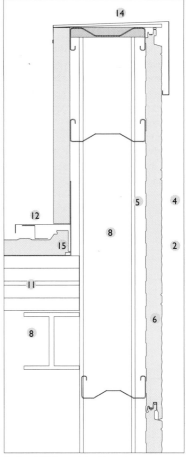

Section 1:10. Parapet at gable end

Details

1. Vertically-set composite panel
2. Horizontally-set composite panel
3. Silicone-based seal
4. Outer metal facing
5. Inner metal facing
6. Inner insulation core
7. Metal capping
8. Supporting structure
9. 4-way interlocking composite panel
10. Fixed light
11. Roof construction, composite panels shown
12. Metal trim
13. Parapet gutter
14. Metal parapet coping
15. Closer strip
16. Door frame

Design considerations

Composite panels comprise a complete wall assembly formed from prefabricated panels provided as proprietary systems. They consist of an inner core of rigid thermal insulation onto which a thin metal sheet is bonded to each side. Their main visual advantage is the smoothness of the panel faces that form a complete system with integral panels for corners, parapets and window openings. Panels are typically made in widths of 1100mm to 1400mm to suit the manufactured width of metal coil but are long, typically up to around 15 metres. Panels typically have interlocking joints on two sides, with the panels being set either vertically or horizontally. Joints between panels at their short ends, where there is no interlocking joint, are butt jointed and sealed with cover strips. Panel systems are also used with interlocking joints on all four sides, and these are usually made in sizes that can easily integrate doors and windows which also form part of proprietary systems.

Vertically-set panels that interlock on two sides are usually storey height. Where panels are stacked over more than one storey, the horizontal joints between panels are usually sealed with metal flashings. Panels are supported on horizontal rails, typically at floor level to allow a floor to ceiling panel arrangement without intermediary structure that would be visible from inside the building. Horizontally-set panels that interlock on two sides are stacked one above the other, with tongue and groove horizontal joints. which usually contrast visually with the vertical joints which have wider sight lines in order to accommodate a metal cover strip, a rubber-based gasket, or their combination.

In four-sided interlocking panels, joints usually incorporate an inner chamber set between an inner and outer seal in order that the system be internally drained and pressure equalised. Window and door frames which interlock into the surrounding panels and are of a depth equal to that of the composite panels. Interlocking joints are usually made sufficiently rigid to allow two or three panels to be used in a storey height without visible supporting structure.

Design solutions

Windows are fitted into both two-sided and four-sided interlocking panels as separate items which do not typically form part of the system. Windows and doors are fitted so that they are either flush with the external face of the panels in order that the same panel to panel flashings can be used to seal the door/window, or alternatively windows/doors are recessed, and metal flashings are used to form the reveal. Some manufacturers offer special corner panels for window reveals which are also used at internal and external corners of the façade.

As part of their proprietary systems, some manufacturers have a range of preformed panels for sills, corners and parapet copings. This avoids the need for visible metal flashings which lap down over the façade to provide a weathertight seal, and have a flatter, smoother appearance when compared to pressed metal flashings. A wider range of interface components is usually available on four-edge interlocking panels to add to the seamless clipped-together appearance of these systems.

Parapets are formed typically with a pressed metal flashing that folds down the face of the façade but can also be created with a parapet panel which can be flat or curved to suit the design. Where a pressed metal flashing is used, thermal insulation is set beneath, with a vapour barrier on the internal (warm in winter) face of the insulation in order to provide continuity of insulation between wall and roof. Colour matching between metal flashing and composite panel is essential to the success of this method, unless a completely different colour is used for folded metal items. Four-edge interlocking systems allow the possibility of a thin parapet coping of around 100mm high in the manner of glazed curtain walling. Any water that penetrates the outer seal is drained away to the base of the wall within the drained and ventilated framing to the panels.

Windows are often given the same colour and finish in order to provide a seamless link between window frame and metal panel, giving the façade the visual crispness of curtain walling rather than that of metal panels. The metal composite panels can also be used to form shutters or solar shading panels attached to the façade as seen in the photograph. Their lightness in weight allows them to be moved easily in adjustable solar shading panels.

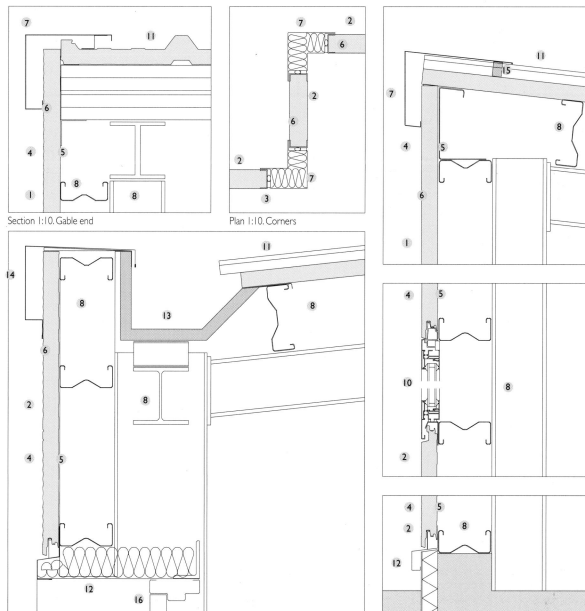

Section 1:10. Gable end

Plan 1:10. Corners

Section 1:10. Parapet with gutter

Section 1:10. Monopitch ridge and window

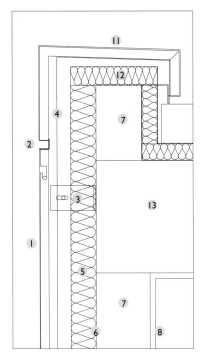

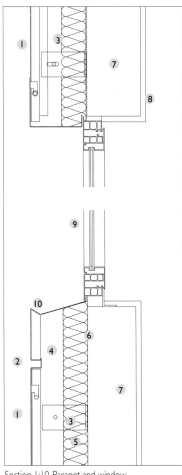

Section 1:10. Parapet and window

Design considerations

In the rainscreen principle, panels with open joints are set forward of a water-proofed backing wall. Wind driven rain that passes through the outer joint is drained away on the outer face of the backing wall. Metal rainscreen panels can have either a completely open joint with framing behind positioned to close views into the void behind, or have folded edges on the panel to close the joint visually, but not to seal it. Small amounts of rainwater that pass through the outer joint are drained away in the ventilated void behind. Visually, this method provides visually crisp joints with strong shadow lines. Narrow joints can give the metal panels a more monolithic appearance as the joints are less visible. Rainscreen panels can provide a flatness or consistency of texture across a façade that is independent of the backing wall behind, with most panels being secured so as to avoid visible fixings. Face fixings on the metal sheet are usually not preferred since, at around 3mm thick, point fixings on a thin sheet can produce visible distortions across the panel surface. Panels are usually formed as trays or 'cassettes' with folded edges that provide both rigidity to the panel and a depth to the joint that both reduces rainwater penetration and obscures views into the void behind. Most panels are fixed with either a hook-on fixing, or with slotted grooves in the manner of composite metal panels that avoid the need for any visible fixings. With hook-on supports, panels have brackets fixed to the sides of the panels that form the tray. Panels are fixed onto vertical rails which are usually aligned with the joints where they serve as a screen to the void behind. Continuous rails are preferred to individual fixings except in small-scale applications, since rails are much faster to fix than individual brackets.

Panel sizes are determined by available metal sheet sizes. Metal coil is supplied typically in 1200mm and 1500mm widths, with metal plate in greater widths and in varying lengths. Metal-faced composite materials are also used, comprising either a thin metal sheet, such as aluminium, bonded to both sides of a rigid plastic core or, alternatively, a single sheet of metal bonded to one side of a honeycomb panel. Composite materials that use a thin (3–5mm) thick inner plastic-based core can be folded to form trays, but honeycomb panels require either an edge strip to conceal the joints, or are set close enough together for

the inner core not to be visible. An alternative method of fixing panels is to form a folded tongue and groove joint on the long edges of the panel where panels slot together. An advantage of this method is that the support framing behind can be simplified with vertically-set or horizontally-set rails to suit the pressed metal panels where concealed fixings can be used.

Design solutions

Façade corners are formed typically either with panels made from folded sheet or thin composite sheet, or alternatively with mitred panels that meet at the corner, particularly where honeycomb panels are used. Internal corners are formed in the same way, but their geometry allows panels to meet without any special panels with two panels butting up to one another.

Parapets are formed in a similar way, with panels that can be fabricated to suit particular project conditions within proprietary systems. Since the coping is sealed between panels on its horizontal face to avoid rainwater falling directly through the joint between panels, the joint is often recessed to match with the open joint on its external vertical face. The coping usually has a little gap between the coping panel and the inner face of the parapet upstand in order to ventilate the cavity, where the joints between the façade panels do not admit sufficient air for ventilation.

Windows in openings are sealed directly against the waterproof layer of the backing wall. The rainscreen panels are terminated adjacent to the window in order to conceal these seals. In order to avoid staining, sills are usually formed in a way that directs rainwater to the sides of the opening and down joints between panels rather than directly down the face of the panels below.

Drips at ground level are formed as pressed metal flashings, with the gap between the panels and the backing wall being closed with metal mesh that allows the passage of air for ventilation but avoids the ingress of insects into the void.

Although manufacturers offer metal rainscreen panel systems, they can be modified to suit individual projects and fabricated economically, since fabrication principles and support systems are well known.

Rainscreen wall assemblies

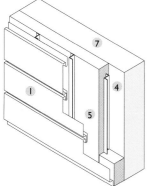

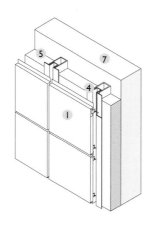

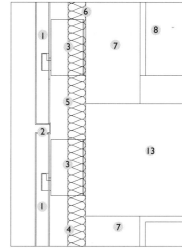

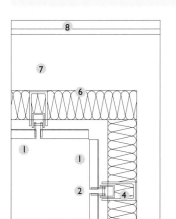

Vineyard, Langenlois, Austria. Architect: Steven Holl

Details

1. Metal rainscreen panel
2. Open joint
3. Support bracket
4. Support frame
5. Closed cell thermal insulation
6. Waterproof membrane
7. Backing wall or structural wall supporting rainscreen
8. Internal finish
9. Window frame inserted into opening in backing wall or structural wall
10. Pressed metal cill
11. Pressed metal coping
12. Continuity of waterproofing layers of wall and roof
13. Structural slab
14. External terrace
15. Ground level

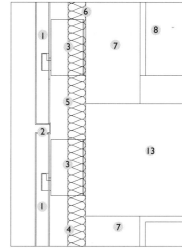

Section 1:10. Panel to panel junction

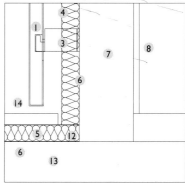

Section 1:10. Roof terrace level

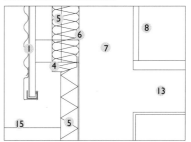

Section 1:10. Ground level

Plan 1:10. Internal corner

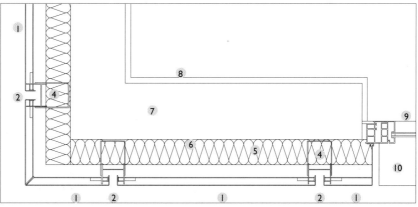

Plan 1:10. External corner

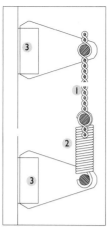

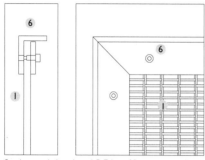

Section 1:5.

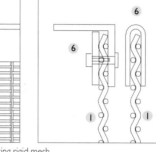

Section 1:5. Edge of frame supporting mesh flexible in one direction. Mesh fixed to patch fittings tensioned by springs on brackets

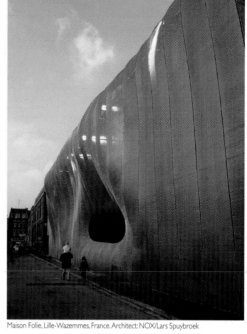

Sections and elevations 1:5. Edge of frame supporting rigid mesh

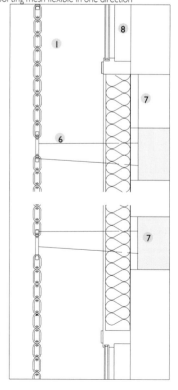

Maison Folie, Lille-Wazemmes, France. Architect: NOX/Lars Spuybroek

Details

1. Stainless steel mesh
2. Stainless steel spring
3. Metal fixing bracket
4. Metal support rod
5. Fixing bolt to tension mesh
6. Metal support edge frame
7. Floor slab or backing wall
8. Adjacent curtain wall

Section and elevations 1:25.
Edge of frame supporting mesh flexible in one direction

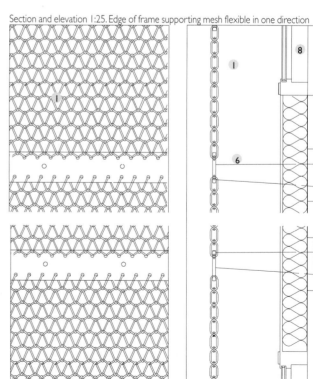

Section and elevation 1:25. Edge of frame supporting mesh flexible in one direction

Design considerations

The use of stainless steel mesh in façades and, more recently, copper mesh, has developed over the past 10 years. From its origins in industrial applications, such as conveyor belts, stainless steel mesh is used in façades for a variety of functions such as solar shading to glazed walls, full height balustrade guarding, and as visual screens to backing walls. The most commonly used type is woven mesh, where stainless steel cables forming part of the mesh can be tensioned at points or along its edges to provide a rigid, lightweight screen that has little visible supporting structure. Stainless steel is preferred to mild steel for its greater durability and resistance to corrosion. Other materials, mainly copper and bronze, are being introduced, but the lower tensile strength of these materials currently limits their use to smaller scale applications. Mesh is of three generic types: fully flexible mesh, mesh flexible in one direction, and rigid mesh.

Fully flexible mesh is made from either a woven metal cloth of strands woven in two directions, or alternatively as thicker wires which are crimped together in a grid. Woven cloth usually has a close weave, with a light transmission range of around 1 per cent to 5 per cent, making it useful where opacity is required, such as solar shading. Metal widths range from around 1800mm to 2400mm and are manufactured in long lengths. More open weave versions are available, which resemble thin cable woven in two directions. These are manufactured in widths of around 6000mm, requiring restraint at around 2000mm centres. The material is held in place by tensioning the material in two directions. Crimped mesh has thin, straight rods running the length of the material, with wire crimped across the width of the material.

Mesh which is flexible in one direction is made from stainless steel cables running the length of the material, with thin stainless steel rods woven into these cables in the opposite direction, across the width of the material. They are manufactured in long lengths, allowing them to be used as a continuous façade 'wrapping' material, either tensioned horizontally across the façade or hung from top to bottom. These meshes are usually made in widths up to around 7500mm but they require restraint at close centres. These materials have a wide variety of weave pattern, giving light transmissions ranging from 25 per cent to 65 per cent. Light transmis-

sion can be reduced by reducing the distance between cables, between rods, or a combination of both, depending on the visual effect required. Cable thicknesses vary from 2mm to 6mm with rod diameters ranging from around 2mm to 4mm. Weave patterns can be as dense as 4mm x 10mm for low light transmission to 20mm x 50mm for high light transmission. Meshes can also incorporate a varying weave within a single length of material to suit varying light transmissions.

Rigid mesh is made from stainless steel rods which are woven in two directions to give a textured appearance. The material is made in relatively small panels of around 1800mm x 1500mm, and is fixed by clamping the materials into a continuous edge frame or by point fixing, since the material cannot be tensioned. The diameter of the rod is typically around 2mm set into a grid of 6mm x 2mm.

Design solutions

Mesh which is flexible in one direction is probably the most widely used type, since the material can be tensioned along its length by the cable ends, which avoids the need for a highly visible supporting frame. Panels can be set by side to create a continuous texture of material. Whether the material is set vertically or horizontally, a similar variety of support methods can be used. The ends of cables can be turned over a continuous rod to form a loop, with the rod being supported on brackets fixed to the supporting structure. Alternatively, the continuous rod can be woven into the mesh, usually during manufacture, with the rod being supported in the same way. Mesh flexible in one direction can also be point fixed, with clips at relatively close centres that are tensioned against a supporting structure. The level of tension can be maintained either with springs, which has been used with point fixed clips, or by a tensioning bolt that retains the supporting rods in position.

Where rigid mesh is fixed into a frame around its edge, the material is usually clamped between flat bars, or angles. The plates are clamped with steel bolts, which can be countersunk to avoid highly visible fixing bolts. The frames are then fixed back to the façade on support brackets. An alternative edge frame is to use a C-shaped folded section into which the rigid mesh is fixed.

Sections and elevations 1:5. Edge of frame supporting mesh flexible in one direction. Mesh is fixed to tensioned rod secured to a metal angle

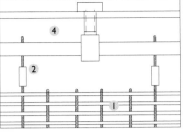

Section 1:5.

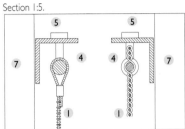

Elevation 1:5.

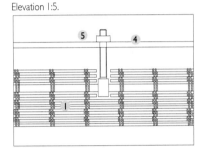

Elevation 1:10.

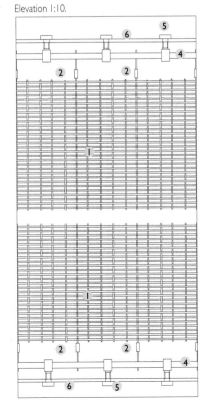

Design considerations

Metal louvres are used typically in façades as terminations to air handling ducts and as solar shading. Metal framed louvres with glass blades are used to provide ventilation to daylit spaces such as semi-open circulation spaces where high levels of thermal insulation are not required. Metal louvre blades are set either vertically or horizontally, usually orientated in a way that avoids views through the blades. At ground/street level, horizontal blades usually conceal views through the void behind, but above ground floor level, the 45° orientation of the blades allows views

through unless an additional bank of blades is added, which both improves weather protection and conceals views through the panel. Vertically set blades provide a screen that conceal views through when seen an oblique angle, but allows views through a small part of the façade when directly facing the façade. Deeper vertically-set blades increase the screening effect for views at close proximity to the louvres. Where more than a single row of inclined blades is needed in horizontally-set louvres, the rainwater is drained at the base of the frame to the outside, or by forming a groove along the bottom edge of each

blade to drain away water through the sides of the louvre frame. Water is then drained to the outside. The perimeter of the frame is sealed against the surrounding waterproofed wall where a different material is used for the surrounding area of façade. Where metal louvres are set into curtain walling systems, blades are set into a perimeter frame to form a complete panel which is then fixed into curtain walling framing in the same manner as a glazed unit or metal panel would be fixed. This is particularly useful where a glazed wall has a few louvre panels that form part of the façade. The louvres can be introduced

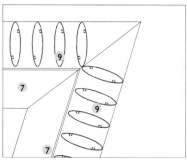

Plan 1:10. Corner of vertically-set extruded aluminium louvres

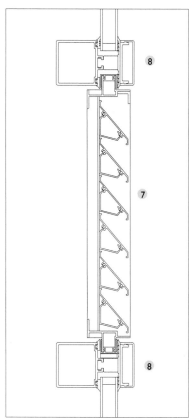

Section 1:5. Horzontally-set extruded aluminium louvres

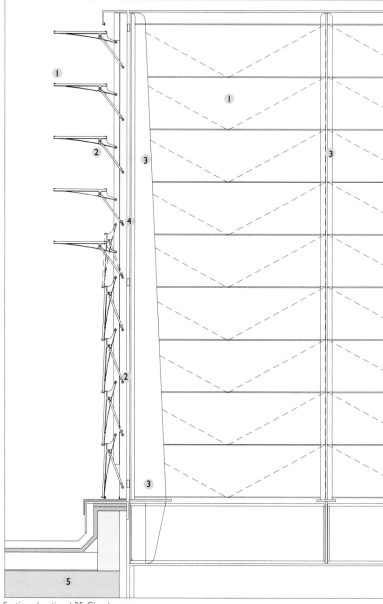

Section, elevation 1:25. Glass louvres

Assembly of vertically-set pivoted louvres with sliding movement mechanism

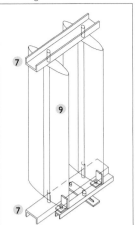

Plans 1:10. Vertically-set extruded aluminium louvres

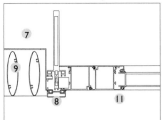

Section 1:10. Louvred door

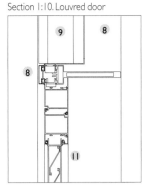

Section 1:10. Vertical louvres.

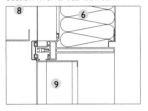

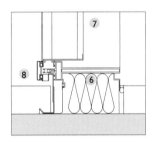

IIT Campus, Chicago, USA. Architect: Office for Metropolitan Architecture

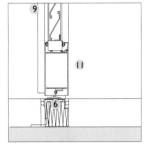

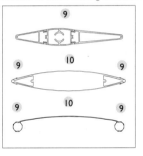

Sections 1:10. Solar shading extrusions

Details to glass louvres
1. Glass louvre blade
2. Extruded aluminium clip supporting louvre blade
3. Supporting structure
4. Extruded aluminium frame
5. Adjacent roof

Details to metal louvres
6. Thermal insulation
7. Extruded aluminium frame
8. Stick curtain walling carrier system
9. Extruded aluminium section
10. Metal sheet
11. Louvre panel door

without the need for changing the system to accommodate the louvres. Water that penetrates the glazing system is drained away through the drained and ventilated cavity of the curtain walling system.

Metal louvre blades are usually made from extruded aluminium in order to provide precise sections that can both encourage the passage of air through the panel as well as minimise rainwater penetration. The blades are fixed into a perimeter frame also formed from extrusions or angle sections (depending on the frame size and drainage method). Panels are fixed into, or forward of, the opening in the façade.

Design solutions

Metal framed louvres with glass blades are finding increased use in façades as part of twin wall configurations, where the outer layer provides solar protection in summer and serves as the outer layer of a thermal buffer in winter. These larger scale louvres

are made in lengths of 1500mm to around 3000mm to suit the modules of glazed curtain walling with which they are used typically. The glass blades are held by clips, usually made in cast or extruded aluminium that provide structural support to the blades. Clips are linked to rods that allow the louvre blades to be opened and closed to suit ventilation and solar shading requirements. The glass used is usually a solar performance type which reduces solar gain but allows the passage of a reduced amount of daylight. Movement of the blades is controlled either manually with a winding mechanism, or electrically, with louvres operated in groups of panels. Panel sizes are around a maximum of 1500mm high × 1200mm wide. Glass blade louvres provide around 70 per cent free area when fully open. Thermal insulation and lower rates of air infiltration can be achieved with double glazed units. The maximum length of panel is also 1200mm, with blade widths of around 150mm to 200mm. Ventilation rates

when open are at around 50 per cent. The high air infiltration rates associated with glass blade louvres have been improved in many years, but are not used where a sealed façade is required.

Metal louvres used for solar shading are set vertically or horizontally to suit the incident sun angles for which shading is provided. Blades can be fixed or be adjustable. Elliptical louvres set on pivots with a sliding arm at the ends to which the blades are connected to provide louvre movement. These can be hand or electrically operated. Aerofoil-type sections can span up to around 3000mm.

Sand trap louvres are used in very dusty and sandy conditions, comprising vertically set interlocking C-shaped profiles that prevent the passage of particles by forcing the air through two changes in direction that traps the sand, causing it to drop to the bottom of the frame and back to the outside.

Developments seen in stick curtain walling have allowed more variety in the expression of framing members, which do not always have to be continuous. Preference for one directional emphasis, as in the Hospital in Madrid by Rafael Moneo shows a mixed use of opaque and vision panels while maintaining a continuous horizontal emphasis to unify the façades. Unitised glazing, particularly the use of silicone-bonded panels, are finding applications in non rectilinear glazing, with panels shaped to suit structural framing that uses a constant size of structural member across a complete wall rather than a hierarchy of primary and secondary members, as illustrated by the Library in Seattle by OMA. Point fixed glazing, both bolt fixed and clamped, is now economic on small projects, and has found considerable use in double skin or 'twin wall' façades where the outer bolt fixed glazing provides an almost continuous volume of glass without a highly visible set of joints as seen in the Control Post in Middelburg, Holland, by BAR.

02_
glass

Photographs. Top (left to right): Pavilion, Son en Breugel, Belgium. Architect: NOX; Control Post, Middelburg, Holland. Architect: BAR Architects; Library, Seattle, USA. Architect: Office for Metropolitan Architecture. Opposite page: Studio, Sydney, Australia. Architect: Glenn Murcutt.

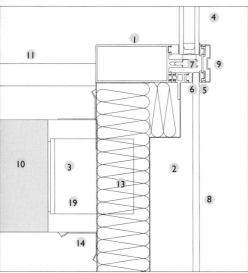

Section 1:5. Junction at floor level

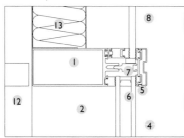

Section 1:5. Junction with glass/metal spandrel panel

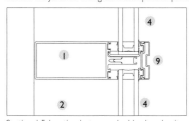

Section 1:5. Junction between double glazed units

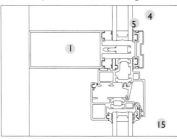

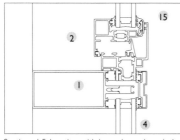

Sections 1:5. Junction with inward opening window

Hospital, Madrid, Spain. Architect: Rafael Moneo

Design considerations

Site-based systems are assembled in place, with each mullion and transom cut to suit and prepared in the factory with the slots and holes required for assembly and installation on site. They suit a wide variety of conditions and complex geometries. Some recent examples allow a discontinuity of mullion and transom (vertical and horizontal framing members) to give a non rectilinear appearance, while maintaining the internally drained and ventilated principles of the system, an essential aspect of this form of glazed wall. Early curtain wall systems suffered from leaks as a result not only of defects in workmanship but of a pressure difference between inside the framing and outside that could draw water into the outer seals. Modern synthetic rubber-based seals to glazed curtain walling accepts that small amounts of water will penetrate the outer seal, and the water is drained away in a chamber immediately behind this seal, and returned to the outside at the base of the wall.

Stick glazing systems comprise extruded aluminium sections onto which double glazed units are set, together with insulated opaque panels, for spandrel conditions, typically faced in metal or opaque glass. Panels are held in place with extruded aluminium pressure plates which secure the panel to the carrier frame with screw type fixings. A synthetic rubber-based outer seal is set between the glass and the pressure plate. A gasket in the same material is also set between the inner face of the panel and the carrier frame to provide an inner air seal. The pressure plate is secured with visible fixings at around 300mm centres,

which are usually concealed with a continuous cover capping, also made from extruded aluminium, which clips onto the pressure plate. The capping profile can be made in a variety of flat, projecting or recessed profiles to suit visual requirements. Similarly, the supporting aluminium grid of mullions and transoms can be formed in a variety of structural-based sections, that can vary from a rectangular box section to an I-section to a T-section with a blade-like appearance.

Stick curtain walling usually spans vertically from floor to floor, where mullion sections are joined with a sliding connection that allows the glazing between each floor level to move independently while maintaining the overall continuity of the system. The movement joint is visible in the façade and is accommodated either at the junction of the mullion and the transom above, or within the length of the transom, usually within the spandrel panel.

The overall continuity of framing in stick glazing ensures that the internal chamber in the transom can drain into an adjacent mullion and that any moisture is drained, typically immediately above movement joints.

Stick glazing is fixed at each floor level, by either hanging it from the top of each mullion and restraining it at the floor level below, or by supporting the mullion at floor level and restraining it at the floor slab above. The hanging mullion option usually allows a smaller mullion to be used, but this depends on the specific application.

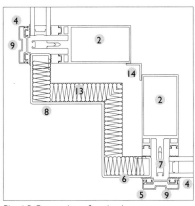

Plan 1:5. Corner above floor level

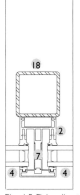

Plan 1:5. Fixing direct
to steel hollow
section

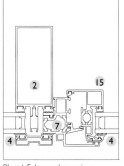

Plan 1:5. Inward opening
window

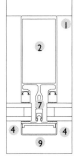

Plan 1:5. Typical
framing using
box section

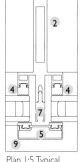

Plan 1:5. Typical
framing using
T-section

Design solutions

Interfaces with openings, edges and different adjacent materials are formed either by the use of metal flashings or by special components that form part of proprietary systems. Windows are fitted by applying an additional sub frame within the main framing against which the opening light is closed. The overall width of the window frame is usually equal to that of the main framing of mullions and transoms. Windows and doors can open outward or inward to suit the design. Electrically operated windows, such as those at high level, usually have a motor in a box that fits within the height of the window frame. The wiring is concealed within the framing.

Junctions at floors are closed by bringing floor finishes up to the transom, which is also set at floor level to close off the gap between floors. The spandrel panel has a smoke seal between separated floors, but a full fire barrier is required in some countries where the spandrel panel is required to be fire resisting and to provide a barrier that stops flames from passing from floor to floor.

Corners are formed, typically, either with a special extrusion that allows a glass to glass junction at the corner, or has two mullions meeting at a corner and an insulated metal flashing turning the corner.

Parapet copings are formed by glazing the bottom edge of the metal flashing into the top transom and folding the flashing over the top of the parapet. Junctions between mullions and adjacent areas of wall in a different material are made in the same way.

Details

1. Transom
2. Mullion
3. Fixing bracket
4. Single / double glazed unit to suit application
5. Pressure plate
6. Synthetic rubber seal
7. Thermal break
8. Metal-faced or opaque glass-faced insulated panel
9. Cover cap
10. Floor slab
11. Floor finish
12. Ceiling finish
13. Thermal insulation
14. Metal sheet seal
15. Opening light
16. Metal honeycomb panel
17. Slot in mullion to receive fixing bracket for external screen
18. Steel hollow section
19. Smoke seal / fire stop
20. Projecting bracket to support external screen

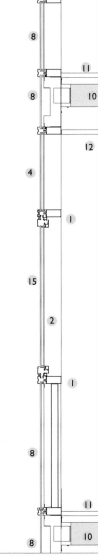

Section 1:25. Typical assembly

Plan 1:5. Corner above floor level

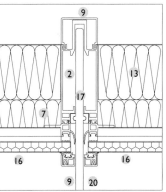

Plan 1:5. External bracket forming penetration

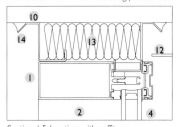

Section 1:5. Junction with soffit

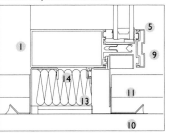

Section 1:5. Junction with floor slab

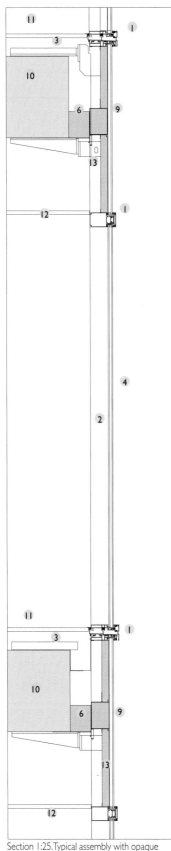

Section 1:25. Typical assembly with opaque spandrel

Design considerations

Like stick glazing, unitised glazing uses aluminium framing to support the glazing, but where stick glazing is secured to a continuous supporting frame all of which is fixed on site, unitised glazing is fabricated as individual panels in the factory. Panels are then lifted into place on site and set next to one another, the gaps between each panel being sealed with synthetic rubber gaskets. Some systems have panels which are completely separate structurally from the adjacent panels, allowing a damaged panel to be removed, either during construction or from later damage. Other systems are semi-interlocking on horizontal joints in order to combine the structural capacity of members as well as assist in internal drainage. The term semi-interlocking is also used for stick systems where large-scale frames, covering several bays both vertically and horizontally are pre-assembled in the factory and then lifted in place on site. The glass units and pressure plates are then fixed on site as per regular stick glazing methods.

In unitised glazing, the double glazed units are fixed to the supporting frame either from the outside of the panel or the inside, to suit the strategy for glass replacement in the event of later damage. The units are secured with pressure plates which are either mechanically fixed to the main frame, or are integral with the frame. An alternative method is to bond the glass units to a sub frame which is then mechanically fixed to the aluminium frame. This method provides an all-glass appearance on the outside, usually with a recessed joint between panels giving a shadow gap appearance between panels.

Vertical joints between panels have an outer seal which is usually formed by two gaskets which are pressed together, either in the form of 'flipper' gaskets or as compressible hollow seals. These are made from synthetic rubber, typically EPDM. Behind this outer seal is a drained and pressure equalised chamber closed off by an inner seal, also formed typically in EPDM. At the internal face of the panel is an air seal. In hot and humid climates, typically in South East Asia, it is assumed that moisture will find its way to the back of the supporting aluminium frame so that moisture is drained from the back of the system. In more temperate climates, the system is sealed in the mid-depth of the framing, with the inner joint, visible from inside the building, serving as an air seal only. Any rainwater that

penetrates the outer seal is drained down through the inner chamber and is expelled at the base of each unitised panel, typically at floor level. Horizontal joints between the transoms formed by the top of one panel and the bottom of the panel above are formed in the same way, with seals aligned with those in the vertical joints to ensure that rainwater is drained to the outside. Unitised panels typically include at least one additional transom to provide a spandrel zone at floor level, for example.

The framing of unitised panels has thermal breaks set within its depth in order to reduce the transmission of heat or cold from the outside of the frame to the inside. The overall width, or sight line, of the unitised panels is greater than those used for stick glazing, from around 80mm to 120mm depending on the application. The greater width often suits the needs of internal partitions, which reach the façade.

Panels are set so that they span from floor slab to floor slab, and like stick glazing, are either hung from a floor slab and restrained on the floor below, or are supported on a floor slab and are restrained on the floor above. Like stick glazing, movement between panels is provided by a sliding spigot joint set into the vertical joint between mullions. This movement is taken out horizontally in the horizontal joint, typically at floor level.

Design solutions

Corner conditions require an additional panel type in order to avoid site assembly in this location. The factory-based fabrication of these panels gives the opportunity for silicone-bonded glazing to be used to provide a frameless corner. The unitised frame is stiffened internally to compensate for the loss of structural stability of the corner. Regular framed corners are made usually with a 45° angled mullion to reduce the visual impact and sight lines of the mullion.

Parapet copings are formed by sealing and waterproofing the gap between the top of the panel and the parapet wall behind with a synthetic rubber seal that is integral with the panel. Thermal insulation is used to provide a complete continuity of insulation from wall to roof. A metal coping is set on top of the panel to provide protection to the membrane beneath.

Plan 1:5. Panel to panel junction at glazing

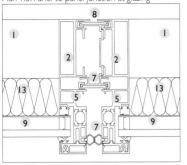

Plan 1:5. Panel to panel junction at spandrel

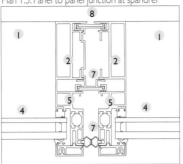

Plan 1:5. Junction with bracket for external screen

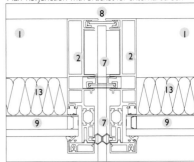

Section 1:5. Panel to panel junction at slab level

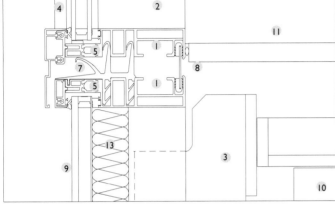

Section 1:5. Panel to panel junction with supporting steel frame

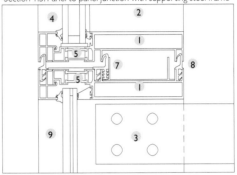

Section 1:5. Intermediate transom

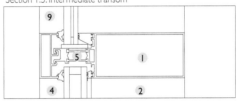

Section 1:5. Intermediate transom at ceiling level

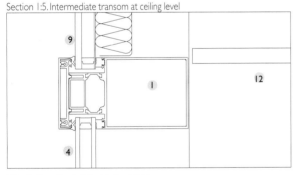

Plan 1:10. Fully unitised glazing

Plan 1:10. Semi-unitised glazing

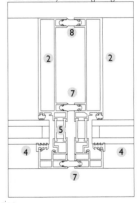

University Library, Utrecht, Holland. Architect: Wiel Arets

Details

1. Transom
2. Mullion
3. Fixing bracket
4. Single/double glazed unit to suit application
5. Thermal break
6. Smoke seal/fire stop
7. Synthetic rubber baffles
8. Synthetic rubber air seal
9. Metal-faced/opaque glass-insulated panels
10. Floor slab
11. Floor finish
12. Ceiling finish
13. Thermal insulation

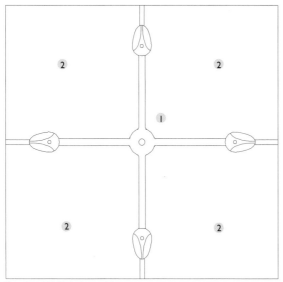

Elevation 1:10. Typical assembly

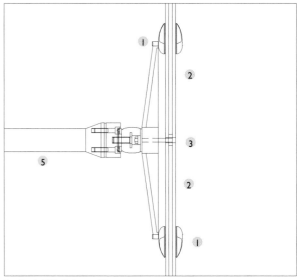

Section 1:10. Typical assembly

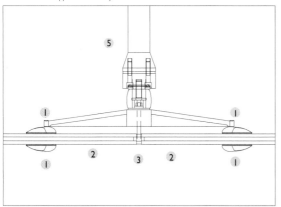

Plan 1:10. Typical assembly

Details
1. Stainless steel patch plates
2. Single glazed or double glazed unit to suit application
3. Silicone seal
4. Supporting rod or cable
5. Support bracket
6. Shoe clamp
7. Glass fin
8. Synthetic rubber gasket

Rheinische Landesmuseum, Bonn, Germany. Architect: Architekten Gruppe, Stuttgart

Design considerations

The two types of point fixed glazing used for façades are clamped glazing and bolt fixed glazing. Both systems are used to increase the transparency of a façade, and this is particularly successful in single glazing, where these methods were first used. Where double glazed units are used with their black edge band and joints between units, the width is usually equal to that of framed glazing, but the omission of framing is still of enormous visual benefit where transparency is required, particularly to oblique views across a façade where the glass is seen as a continuous uninterrupted surface, made all the more dramatic where curves and folds in the glass surface are used.

In clamped glazing, the fixings holding the plates in place usually pass through the joints between the glass to avoid the additional complexity and cost of drilling the glass. Because fixings are positioned at the glass edges, rather than within the glass itself, the span between fixings is higher than for an equivalent bolt fixed solution and glass thicknesses may be higher for a clamped glazing solution as a result.

Single clamped glazing is used primarily in the outer glazed wall in a twin wall configuration, where the glass is joined with stainless steel clamps, plates and brackets. The use of plates allows a more complex geometry of glass to be used, such as in a shingled arrangement of lapped glass panels. In this arrangement, air can pass up through gaps between lapped glass sheets while admitting only small amounts of rainwater into the buffer zone behind. Glass can be supported either at the

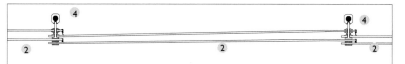

Plans 1:25. Panels in lapped arrangement (above) and in vertically-aligned arrangement (below)

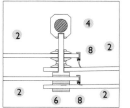

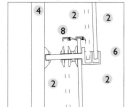

Plan 1:10. Junction at panel-to-panel   Section 1:10. Junction at panel-to-panel

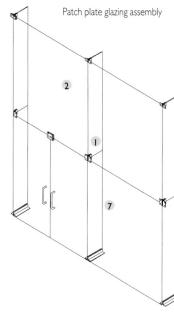

Patch plate glazing assembly

corners, or along its edges to suit the supporting structure for the glass, which is usually visually lightweight in order to maximise transparency. Clamps are formed by setting a synthetic rubber gasket, typically EPDM, between the stainless steel plate and the glass sheet. A bolt is passed through one side of the bolt and is secured into the other plate, usually with a countersunk type.

Patch plate glazing uses metal brackets that secure glass panels to glass fins that provide structural stability to an all-glass façade. Glass fins are set at 90° to the plane of the glass, typically fixed back to either to the floor or the slab above. Glass fins are usually in lengths equal to the height of each panel, with a patch plate connection occurring at each horizontal joint of the glass, to form a single structural section. Glass panels and fins are joined with cleats and plates at the corner junctions, and are usually fixed through holes in the glass rather than through the joints in order to transfer loads effectively through the plates. Clamping plates usually have a polished or brushed finish to allow them to be cleaned easily to avoid surface discoloration.

With double glazed clamped glazing the use of the joint between units to pass fixings is important in order to avoid the cost of drilling glass that is required with bolt fixed systems. Double glazed units are beginning to be used in a lapped configuration, with the use of synthetic rubber gaskets to provide seals, set within the depth of the glass unit perimeter to avoid them being seen in elevation from either side of the glass.

Design solutions

Patch plate glazing with glass fins is usually set into a glazing channel at floor level in order to allow the glass to be seen terminating at floor level. The base of structural glass fins supported at floor level rather than the ceiling are usually set below the floor finish in order to conceal the patch plate brackets, which are usually set either within the floor finishes zone or within a pocket in the floor slab where this zone is insufficiently deep. The same principle is used where the fin is hung from the ceiling. Patch plates are also used to support doors giving a continuous appearance to the façade. Doors are set typically on floor springs, set into the floor, and are supported at the top of the door leaf with a pivot which is clamped to the glass unit above.

Clamped glazing is usually able to accommodate higher amounts of structural movement than an equivalent framed glazing system, which has encouraged the use of tensioned cables, usually set vertically, to which the glass is fixed. Cables are usually set immediately behind vertical joints to reduce their number and visibility, since plates offset from the vertical joint require either an additional vertically-set cable, or an additional metal bracket to connect the two patch plates back to a single cable. In supporting cable structures, which allow higher amounts of structural movement, doors are required to be set independently of the glazed wall, usually with a metal frame around the opening which is fixed at floor level only, and is structurally independent of the glazed wall.

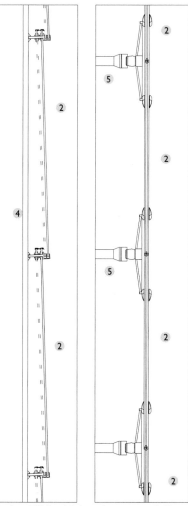

Sections 1:25. Panels in lapped arrangement (left) and in vertically-aligned arrangement (right)

Reflex HQ, Treviso, Italy. Architect: Cesare Monti-Gemini Studio

Details

1. Cast or plate steel connector
2. Outside
3. Single / double glazed unit to suit application
4. Silicone seal
5. EPDM extrusion
6. Supporting steel tube
7. Bolt fixing
8. Steel connector rod secured to primary structure
9. Stainless steel cable shown as support
10. Concrete floor slab
11. Insulated metal panel

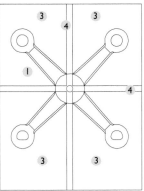

Elevation 1:10. X-shaped fixing   Section 1:10. X-shaped fixing

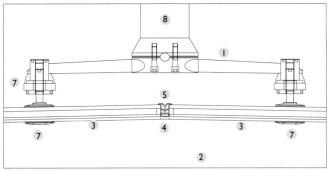

Plan 1:10. Corner with bolt fixings supporting on cable net structure.

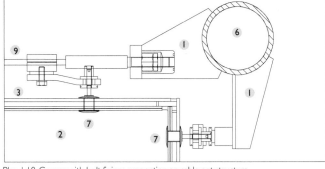

Plan 1:10. H-shaped fixing.

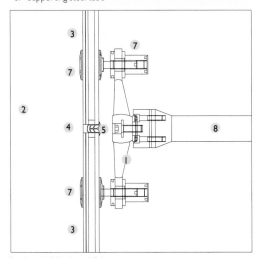

Section 1:10. H-shaped fixing.

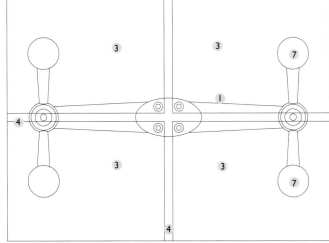

Elevation 1:10. H-shaped fixing.

Design considerations

In common with clamped glazing, this method is used for its transparency, but usually with smaller visible fixings. Like clamped glazing, it was originally developed for single glazing, but is more commonly used with double glazed units, with their 50mm joint width, including the edge of unit. Despite the overall 50mm black joint width, the absence of framing and continuity of the reflective surface of glass makes this frameless system more visually lightweight than framed glazing. The bolt fixings used are usually smaller than the equivalent clamp fixings, which are set at the joints between the glass. The use of bolt fixings set within the glass rather than at its edges allows glass to be thinner than the clamped version.

Like other clamped glazing systems, bolt fixed glazing is either hung from the top of the wall, or is supported at its base. In hung systems, the glass is fixed onto cables or rods which are suspended from the top and tensioned at the bottom. This allows a visually lightweight supporting structure to be used, but which requires lateral stability to overcome the higher deflections associated with single cables. This higher deflection is usually overcome either by forming a vertically-set cable truss from the primary cable supporting the glass units, or by adding horizontal outriggers from structural columns to restrain the horizontal movement of the cables. Bottom supported systems usually use glass fins or mild steel posts to support the glazing. Glass fins are fixed perpendicular to the vertical joints between glazed units, with an L-shaped bracket and bolt fixing at each end. Glass panels are stacked one above the other, using the glass fins to provide lateral support. Glass fins can also be fixed at the top of the wall or at ceiling level, where they serve as stiffeners in a downstand condition, with the glass still being supported at its base. Glass fins have clamps fixed to them as per the patch plate system described in the previous section.

Where steel posts are used in place of glass fins, glazed units can be bolt fixed individually back to the post, so that all the loads of the glazed units are taken on the posts rather than through the glass. The metal brackets supporting the glass are usually larger than those required for other methods of support. The steel posts can also be formed as trusses, typically with cables and tube sections in order to reduce the visual impact of the supporting structure.

Design solutions

For both top hung and bottom supported methods of bolt fixed glazing, a similar fixing bolt is used which varies according to the required appearance, the size of the glass panel it carries, and the way it connects to the supporting structure. The bolt fixing is the mechanical connection which is fixed through a hole formed in the glass sheet or double glazed unit. Bolts can have a disc fixed to each external face of the glass, be countersunk to be flush with the outer face of the glass, or penetrate only the inner glass of a double glazed unit. Structural movement and deflections between the supporting structure and the glass are accommodated with a rotating swivel connection at the junction of the bolt fixing that passes through the glass and the end of the threaded rod that projects forward of the glass which is connected to the supporting structure. The rotating joint is allowed to move around 12° in all directions away from its regular position.

The bolt fixing is secured to connectors whose shape suits the geometry of the intersection of four bolt fixings at a panel intersection. In small-scale applications, connectors can be a simple steel angle, with one side supporting the bolt fixing and the other side fixed to the supporting column, or truss, for example. Larger-scale applications typically use X-shaped or H-shaped connectors to suit the position of bolts set around the intersection of four glass panels. Connectors are made as either castings or machined/welded components depending on the quantity required and their complexity of form. Where several parts are required to be welded and machined, it is usually more economic and visually preferable to use a casting.

Corners in façades can be made by projecting the glazed wall beyond their points of support to form a cantilevered glass corner, and linking the glass panels together with bolt fixings in a pin connection. Alternatively supporting structure is introduced in the corner, with bolt fixings being attached to a structural member. Where a cantilevered junction is used, manufacturers increasingly provide a limited range of standard components, though it is not uncommon for special connections to be provided for each project.

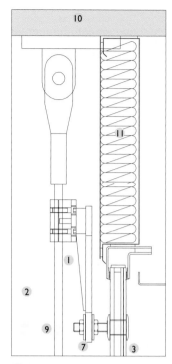

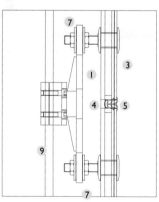

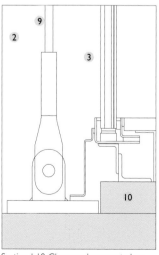

Section 1:10. Glass panels supported on cables or rods

Fashion Centre, Fukuoka. Japan. Architect: Takamatsu Architects and Associates

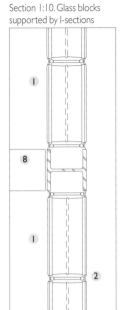

Section 1:10. Glass blocks supported by I-sections

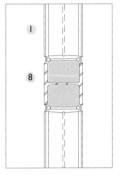

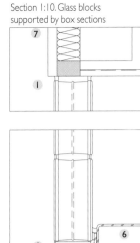

Section 1:10. Glass blocks supported by box sections

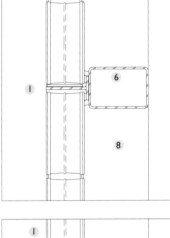

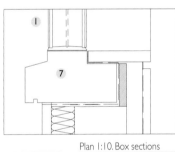

Plan 1:10. Box sections

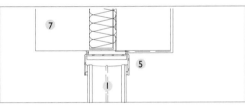

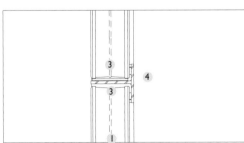

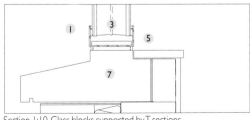

Section 1:10. Glass blocks supported by T-sections

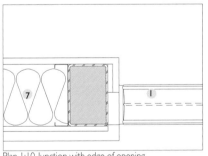

Plan 1:10. Junction with edge of opening

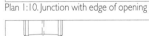

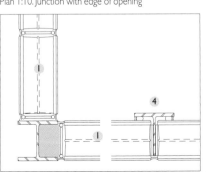

Plans 1:10. Glass blocks supported by T sections and I-sections

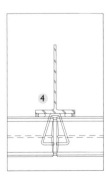

Design considerations

Glass blocks provide a robust, fire resisting translucent glazed wall. They are made as both solid and hollow blocks, with the hollow type giving greater thermal insulation and acoustic insulation. The most common block sizes are a nominal 200mm x 200mm and 300mm x 300mm, generally 100mm thick. Blocks are set in stack bonded rectilinear grids within panels, which are formed either as openings in walls or as bays of a structural frame, usually in reinforced concrete or steel. The continuous vertical and horizontal joints of these non-loadbearing panels give the appearance of glazing rather than a masonry wall, but panel sizes are limited from around 3600mm x 3600mm in area, to around 4500mm x 4500mm in area, depending on block thickness. The panel size can be adjusted in proportion to give a maximum height of around 6000mm and a maximum width of around 7500mm.

Glass blocks are particularly well suited to providing an economic fire resisting glazed construction. One hour fire resisting panels can be made in panel sizes of around 3000mm x 3000mm in area, with a maximum height or width of 4000mm. Panels providing fire resistance greater than 60 minutes, usually up to 90 minutes, require metal channel restraints at the perimeter of the panel due to their greater reliability than cement mortar or silicone seals.

The relatively poor thermal insulation when compared with double glazed units can lead to condensation occurring on the interior face of the block, and adequate ventilation is required to avoid this. Consequently, their use remains more suited to semi-external conditions in temperate climates, such as circulation spaces. Glass block panels fixed into reinforced concrete frames or wall openings are bedded in either mortar or silicone, with flexible joints introduced on the sides and top edge to allow for structural movement. Glass blocks are set within the frame which forms the external wall, or on the edge of reinforced concrete floor slabs. Storey height panels on the edge of floor slabs require metal angle restraints at the top of the opening to accommodate the deflection in the slab. This can be overcome by setting the glass blocks forward of the floor slab on a steel frame in the manner of glazed curtain walling.

Glass blocks can also be set into steel frames made from I-sections, box sections, T-sections or a combination of these. In smaller openings, a T-section is set into joints to stiffen the panels at mid height between floor and ceiling/soffit. Larger panels can be formed by adding a rectangular box section to the back edge of the T-section to form a complete structural frame.

Cast glass channels can also be used for their qualities of providing a long spanning material with fewer joints. Channels resemble half glass blocks in section, manufactured in lengths up to around 2500mm. Most are made around 250mm wide and 60mm deep. Channels are set either vertically or horizontally in a single layer, or can be interlocked by setting channels facing one another to form a double layer with smooth internal and external appearance. The interlocked version also provides a U-value similar to that of hollow glass blocks.

Design solutions

Glass blocks require bed reinforcement between joints, usually provided by a metal ladder-type reinforcing strip which is set within the joints and is not visible. Silicone is also used to bond blocks, with a sealing silicone used on the external face to provide a weathertight seal. Cement-based mortars are also used, with the choice of material being governed largely by visual considerations. Corners are formed usually with either the structure that supports the panel or special corner panels which form a part of most proprietary systems, mainly 90° and 45° corners. Junctions of blocks with adjacent walls are formed with a flexible seal, either silicone-based or with metal angle restraints. The angles are usually concealed by wall finishes, both internally and externally. Flexible seals are used where a door or window opening is introduced into a glass block wall. The door is usually fixed at its base only in order to allow the block wall to be structurally independent, but sometimes the door is tied into the horizontal joints of the glass block wall.

Cast glass channels are fixed into aluminium extrusions at their ends, and are sealed with silicone-based seals between long joints. Vertically-set channels can be bottom supported, but in horizontally-set arrangements, each channel is individually supported rather than each channel being supported on the one below.

Details

1. Glass block
2. Bedding reinforcement
3. Bedding compound, mortar or silicone-based bond
4. Steel flat or T-section
5. Metal edge frame
6. Steel box section
7. Enclosing wall or adjacent wall
8. Steel support frame
9. Cast glass channel

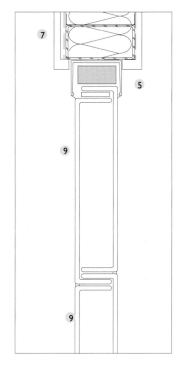

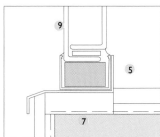

Section 1:10. Cast channels in metal frame

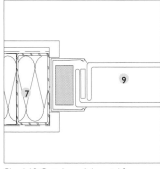

Plan 1:10. Cast channels in metal frame

Matsunoyama Natural Science Museum, Japan. Architect: Tezuka Architects

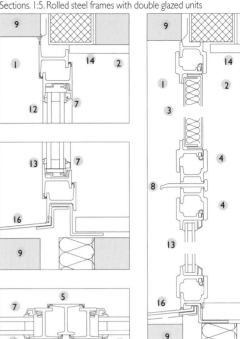

Plans 1:5. Rolled
steel frames with
double glazed units

Details

1. Outside
2. Inside
3. Fixed metal faced panel
4. Rolled steel transom
5. Rolled steel mullion
6. Single / glazed unit to suit application
7. Glazing bead (rolled or pressed)
8. Projecting transom
9. Surrounding wall

Design considerations

The main advantage of rolled steel window frames is their thin sight lines when compared to those in aluminium for small-scale window openings, but the thermal performance of the frames is considerably lower, due to the difficulty of introducing a thermal break into small sections. Larger scale steel curtain walling, used mainly for its fire resisting qualities, can incorporate a thermal break but its sightlines are similar to those of an equivalent aluminium curtain walling system. Steel windows are either fitted into wall openings or are joined together to form a window wall deeper sections.

Small scale steel windows with double glazed units are made with rolled steel sections to form windows of a maximum size of around 3000mm x 1800mm down to a minimum size of 250mm x 400mm. These windows do not have a thermal break. Larger-scale steel curtain walling has a grid of pressed steel mullions and transoms to which double glazed units are fixed with steel pressure plates. Seals are provided with synthetic rubber gaskets similar to those used in aluminium curtain walling systems. Single glazed units have small channels or angle shaped glazing beads to hold the glass in place, while double glazed units usually have extruded clips that hold the glass in place.

Larger windows and doors are made in pressed steel sections in sizes similar to an equivalent in aluminium but have the advantage of providing fire resisting glazing that includes a thermal break. Unlike aluminium windows, where new extrusions can be made economic for each project, pressed and rolled sections for steel windows cannot produce new sections as easily. Window walls are made by fixing individual windows into a stiffening frame of rolled steel T-sections or box sections.

Design solutions

Outward opening lights for both windows in rolled and pressed sections have profiles that lap over the front of the surrounding fixed frame, with a drip above the window to avoid rainwater finding its way in through the top of the frame. Any water that finds its way into the frame is drained down the sides of the frame and out at the bottom. Most windows have synthetic rubber seals to both assist drainage and reduce air infiltration through the opening light.

With inward opening lights the top of the window is protected by the top transom of the fixed frame. The window is more vulnerable at its bottom edge where it is protected by a projecting sill.

Doors are constructed in the same way, but with horizontal rails to provide greater stiffness where rolled sections are used, and thicker horizontal sections in doors where pressed steel sections are used.

Corners are formed with either T-sections

that meet to form a recessed corner, or with a square-shaped hollow section to form a solid corner.

Larger-scale glazing has framing with a continuous indented groove that forms a channel into which toggle-type fixings are inserted to receive the fixings that secure the pressure plates. The synthetic rubber seals on either side of the glass provide a sealed chamber behind the pressure plate which is used to drain away any water that penetrates the outer line of defence. This void is ventilated, with transoms draining water at the base of each glazed unit using a synthetic rubber strip

that slopes down to drain water to the outside.

Parapets are formed by glazing a folded metal coping into the top transom (horizontal) and folding it over the parapet behind. Corners are framed with either glazed or glass-to-glass corners in the manner of aluminium curtain walling but where the glazing is fire resistant, panel sizes are limited.

Metal flashings and an EPDM foil behind it are also used to seal steel glazing against areas of adjacent construction such as masonry and concrete walls. Opening lights and doors are set into steel glazing as separate items

glazed within an opening. As with aluminium glazed walls, opening lights have an additional frame which is visible from the outside. Door and window lights are formed from pressed steel sections which are folded together to form a family of profiles to suit different sizes and glass types. Steel framed windows and doors are also made as separate items for glazing into openings in masonry walls. In this instance they are fixed through the frame into the adjacent structural wall. An EPDM foil or silicone sealant is then used to seal the gap between the steel window/door and the adjacent wall.

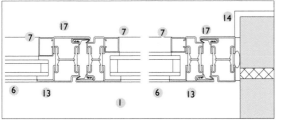

Plan 1:5. Pressed steel windows, thermally broken

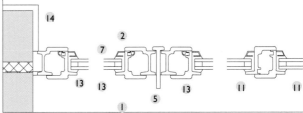

Plan 1:5. Rolled steel frames glazed internally

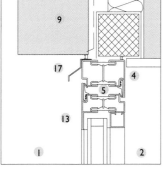

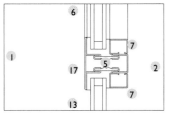

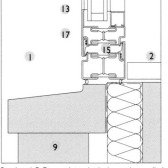

Section 1:5. Pressed steel windows, thermally broken

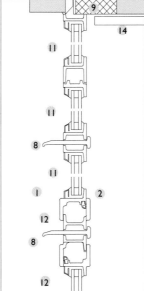

Section 1:5. Rolled steel frames glazed externally

Details *continued*
10. Synthetic rubber seal
11. Fixed light
12. Inward opening light
13. Outward opening light
14. Internal finish
15. Thermal break
16. Steel cill
17. Pressed steel glazing section
18. Pressed steel pressure plate

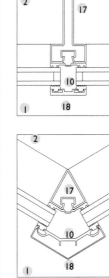

Plans 1:5. Steel framed curtain walling

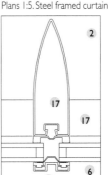

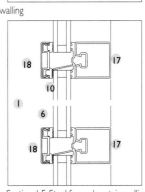

Section 1:5. Steel framed curtain walling

Plans 1:10. Windows set into a glazed rainscreen

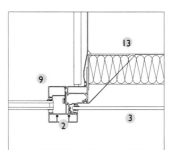

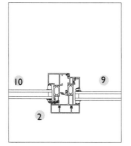

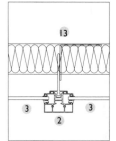

Plans 1:10. Inward opening window/door

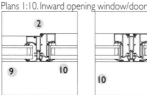

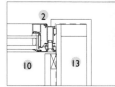

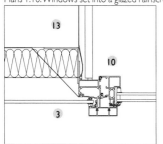

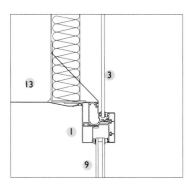

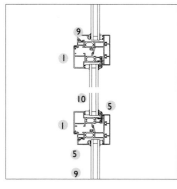

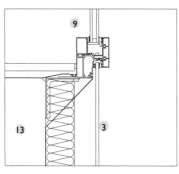

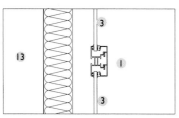

Sections 1:10. Windows set into a glazed rainscreen

Design considerations

Aluminium windows are used either as separate lights in structural openings or as a complete window wall where individual lights in structural openings are linked by opaque panels to give the appearance of an overall modular glazed façade. In contrast to curtain walling, which is a structurally independent external wall, window walls have windows fixed into a structural wall or backing wall, with infill panels that are fixed back to that wall. Window walls provide the appearance of a curtain wall combined with the acoustic and fire resisting properties of its backing wall, making it suitable for apartments, for example.

The main advantages of aluminium windows over other those in other materials is their thermal insulation properties combined with low rates of air infiltration when compared to other materials. The main disadvantage is the wide sight lines required structurally and in accommodating seals for internal drainage and thermal breaks. Where sight lines are reduced, the depth of windows are increased correspondingly to maintain structural stability. Like aluminium curtain walling, aluminium windows are pressure equalised and internally drained in order to provide two lines of defence against rainwater penetration. An outer seal, typically a synthetic rubber 'flipper' type gasket, excludes most of the rainwater, but any water that passes through is drained away at the bottom of the profile to the outside. The internal barrier serves as an air seal rather than as a full weather tight seal as wind-blown rain is stopped by the outer seal. An additional function of the flipper gasket is to provide a continuity with the thermal break so

that the air temperature of the inner chamber is much closer to the internal temperature than the external temperature. In recent years both opening lights and door leafs have thermal breaks incorporated into their frames, which was previously not always the case.

Where window frames tend to be narrower and deeper in section, in order to accommodate the seals and thermal breaks, doors are usually wider in order to provide greater stiffness for the glazed units which they support. Doors are not usually thermally broken since rigidity and durability of the frame is usually the most important consideration. Doors with lower air infiltration rates and a thermal break are made from window sections rather than door sections. The increased performance usually results in smaller maximum door sizes, at around 2400mm for a thermally broken, internally drained and ventilated door. Doors with thermal breaks can reach a maximum of around 3000mm to 3500mm without wide sight lines. Doors with thermal breaks can exceed 2400mm high by silicone bonding the glass to the frame so that glass assists in stiffening the frame. The maximum width of doors are a function of its height, in order to restrict the overall weight, but a 850mm wide door leaf for a 1700mm wide pair of doors is not uncommon. Minimum door width is about 250mm for a double glazed unit. Minimum heights of glazed ventilators, such as those set above doors for night time ventilation, is around 750mm to suit the needs of the opening mechanism. Side hung, top hung, bottom hung and tilt/turn windows use similar aluminium profiles.

Frieder Burda Museum, Baden Baden, Germany. Architect: Richard Meier

Sections 1:10. Aluminium windows fixed into masonry / concrete walls

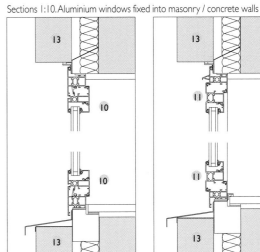

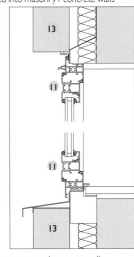

Plans 1:10. Aluminium windows fixed into masonry / concrete walls

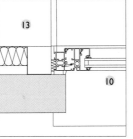

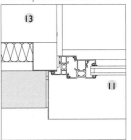

Section 1:10. Outward opening door

Section 1:10. Inward opening door.

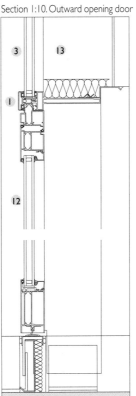

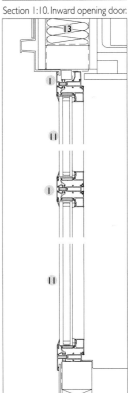

Design solutions

Windows and doors are sealed at their interface with the surrounding walls usually with a synthetic rubber strip which forms an integral part of the window frames, or alternatively with a seal between window frame and opening, typically with a silicone-based product. Some synthetic rubber seals have a metal facing, for additional protection, called a 'foil'. These seals are usually concealed by the adjacent wall construction. The EPDM-foil seal is used where the window is fitted first, since the surrounding wall must be clear in order to fix it, and a perimeter seal is usually used where the window is fitted after the adjacent external wall has been completed.

Aluminium window walls have infill panels that are opaque, in order to both conceal and protect the backing wall behind. Metal panels or opaque glass is often used, with metal panels in rainscreen configuration, and screen printed glass. The opaque panels are fitted to a simple support as required by rainscreens and composite panels rather than a full curtain walling system.

Windows are set forward of the opening where the complete façade is required to be set in a single plane, rather than within the opening itself. The gap between window and opening is closed with metal flashings, which can be concealed with internal finishes.

Details

1. Extruded transom
2. Extruded mullion
3. Fixed metal or opaque glass panel
4. Single / double glazed unit to suit application
5. Synthetic rubber seal
6. Glazing bead
7. Thermal break
8. Silicone-based seal
9. Fixed light
10. Inward opening light
11. Outward opening light
12. Outward opening door
13. Surrounding wall

Windows are not technically inferior to curtain walling, but are a different method of glazing. Window systems are well suited to apartments, where the discontinuity of framing is preferred for acoustic reasons, avoiding flanking sound passing from apartment to apartment. 'Window walls' of windows linked by glass or metal panels is often preferred where a fire separation zone is needed between apartments, when combined with thermal and acoustic mass.

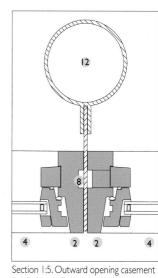

Section 1:5. Outward opening casement in window wall

House, Ste Marguerite de la Masson, Quebec, Canada. Architect: Saia Barbarese Topouzanov

Plan 1:5. Fixed casement in window wall

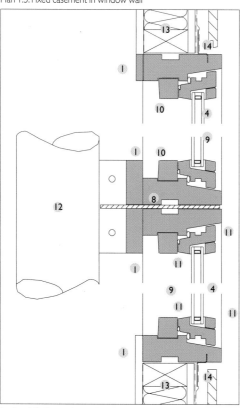

Section 1:5. Outward opening casement in window wall

Details

1. Transom
2. Mullion
3. Fixed light
4. Outward openinglight
5. Vertical sliding sash
6. Head
7. Cill
8. Metal stiffener
9. Single / double glazed unit to suit application
10. Fixing bead
11. Synthetic rubberseal
12. Supporting struc-ture (steel shown)
13. Adjacent wall
14. Metal flashing

In the photo above, the House by Saia Barbarese Topouzanov has windows and doors that have frames built into the timber framed walls that surround them. This gives the window frames both narrow sight lines, where required, and wider lines where the mass of the timber frame is required to be expressed to contrast with the smooth planes of opaque wall.

Design considerations

In common with aluminium windows, timber windows are used either individually within wall openings or are located together to form a complete 'window wall'.

Window walls are formed by linking windows into a continuous arrangement, and reinforced by a secondary frame, such as steel flats or, alternatively, are formed as a complete curtain walling system.

Where individual windows are linked together with reinforcing plates, the panel size is limited and the window wall arrangement is fixed back to the supporting structure of floor slabs or supporting wall. Steel tubes, T-sections or box sections are used where the visual mass of an equivalent timber section is not preferred. These reinforcements are visually set within the construction to avoid being exposed to the effects of the weather. In addition, the high moisture movement associated with timber makes penetrations through the external face of the timber glazed wall more difficult to waterproof.

Where windows are linked and reinforced with a mild steel flat, a drainage groove in the joint ensures that any water that penetrates the outer joint is drained away to the outside at the bottom of the window or window wall. Drainage channels are used on all four sides of the window in the manner of aluminium curtain walling. The steel stiffening rib or bracket does not extend forward of the drainage groove to allow water to be drained away unimpeded. Mullions and transoms (verticals and horizontals) may be of different depth to suit their individual structural requirements and may be in a different wood.

Plans 1:5. Outward opening window (top, side or bottom hung) in window wall with different framing methods

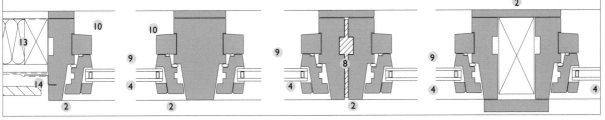

Plans 1:5. Vertical sliding sash window

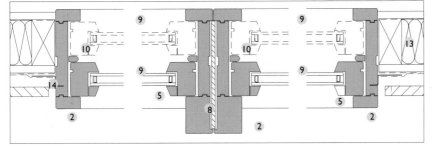

Sections 1:5. Vertical sliding sash window

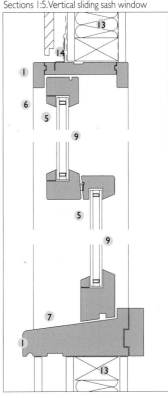

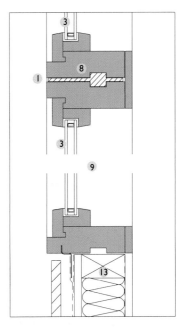

Hardwoods and softwoods can be mixed in a single window wall construction, but the relative moisture movements associated with each type is taken in account to ensure that this movement does not adversely affect the appearance or stability of the window wall.

Timber framed window walls typically span up to two floors, due to the self weight of the panels. This is due to the need to tie the frame into large single units to avoid the effects of thermal movement from either shrinking of the sections. If timber sections are not tied together, they tend to warp and twist when exposed to outside elements. Even if the surfaces are painted or sealed with varnish, any movement due to moisture will crack the outer finish and allow further movement to occur. Timber sections are jointed with either tongue-and-groove or rebated joints. Where tongue-and-groove joints are used, the linking material can be a durable hardwood or aluminium. Sections can also be bolted together if the sections are of sufficient size, such as around 75mm x 50mm.

Design solutions

Timber glazed walls can be sealed against adjacent wall construction with metal flashings that are sealed to the surrounding wall. Corners can be formed with either a timber post forming the corner or as a fully glazed junction. Where transoms meet at a corner without the benefit of a mullion (vertical) the junction is usually joined with a toothed junction to ensure that no visible movement occurs. The full interlocking connection between components in these exposed conditions is vital to the success of timber glazed walls.

Timber windows can achieve low levels of air infiltration and have vastly improved in their weather performance in recent years. Overall performance has been enhanced by the use of synthetic rubber seals and aluminium weather bars. Weather tightness has been enhanced by the use of pressure equalised rebates in the window section so that any water that finds its way beyond the outer seal is drained away without being drawn through by capillary action as a result of an air pressure difference between inside and outside the framing. The inner synthetic rubber seal also serves as an acoustic barrier, providing increased sound insulation. Seals between the window and the opening have been improved in recent years with the increased use of folded aluminium and UPVC profiles which are set into a groove around the window during manufacture and are sealed against the surrounding wall.

There has been an increased control of moisture movement of the timber used with better controlled kiln-drying. Treatments to timbers are also changing to avoid toxic run-off while providing protection against insect attack and the effects of colour fading from UV radiation from sunlight. Some more economic timber windows which have traditionally suffered from poor jointing at the corners of the frame, have been improved with the use of double mortise and tenon joints and enhanced wood glues.

The use of reinforced concrete loadbearing walls as, visually, a hybrid between an opaque loadbearing wall and framed construction. Part of the success of this method is the ability to form glazed panels with very close dimensional control to suit complex shapes of openings in the concrete, as at Tod's in Tokyo by Toyo Ito. Although close dimensional control is now taken for granted in fully glazed systems, this advantage can now be used for individually fixed panels or windows within an exposed finish reinforced concrete wall. The possibilities of this cast material to form ever-more complex shapes with a self-finish is being exploited in GRC (glass reinforced concrete), where varying profiles (in section) and non-rectilinear openings can be formed with relative ease, as seen at Kashiwanoha-Campus Station, Japan by Makoto Sei Watanabe. Precast concrete panel which interlock in the manner of metal composite panels have found greater popularity with their advantage of being checked for visual quality and consistency before delivery to site.

03_
concrete

Photographs. Top (left to right): Tod's, Tokyo, Japan. Architect: Toyo Ito, Kashiwanoha-Campus Station, Japan. Architect: Makoto Sei Watanabe.
Opposite page: Tod's, Tokyo, Japan. Architect: Toyo Ito

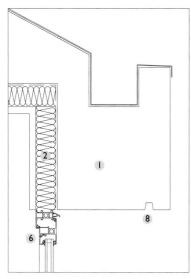

Section 1:10. Loadbearing concrete wall with insulation set on internal face

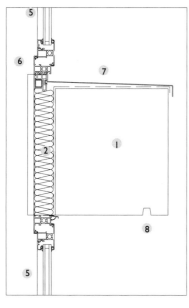

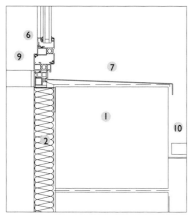

Design considerations

This section on cast in situ loadbearing walls discusses the technique used with an exposed concrete finish rather than as a backing wall to a different façade system. The method of forming concrete by pouring it between formwork makes its construction quite different to working with other materials. Where metal, glass, timber and masonry are made in relatively small panel and unit sizes, concrete is restricted primarily by the available formwork and the amount that can be poured at one time.

The position of the insulation within the construction affects the use of the thermal mass of concrete and its ability to contribute to night-time cooling. Continuity of thermal insulation is increasingly important in the interface of concrete with glazed openings and doors in order to avoid thermal bridging. An important development in recent years has been an increase in setting thermal insulation within the depth of the construction, allowing the external face to have a visible concrete finish. In this wall construction, diaphragm walls are used with two walls linked structurally being set either side of a rigid thermal insulation core. This allows part of the concrete structure to remain closer to the internal temperature of the building, benefit from the thermal mass of the building, as well as permitting the internal face of the building to have a visible concrete finish.

An alternative method of constructing an in situ cast concrete wall is to set the thermal insulation on the inside face of the wall, but at the loss of the thermal mass presented by the construction. This method has the advantage of economy, especially where the thermal mass of the wall is not required to be used.

In diaphragm walls, the two linked concrete walls are joined structurally by strips of concrete which form limited thermal bridges, or alternatively are linked by stainless steel ties. The use of metal ties avoids the thermal bridging with its associated risk of condensation and pattern staining forming on the inside of the wall in temperate climates.

Design solutions

Dust and dirt that settles on horizontal or slightly sloping surfaces such as window cills is washed off during rain and can be deposited on adjacent areas of wall. For this reason, the detailing of openings, parapets and cills in exposed concrete walls ensures that rainwater is thrown as clear as possible from the external wall surface. Projecting cills and flashings are used for this purpose. In urban areas, dust-catching wall textures are usually avoided and smooth finishes are often preferred. However, where protective treatments are applied to the external surface of the concrete to reduce porosity, this can give a reflectivity to the material that takes away its characteristic stone-like appearance.

Drips are cast into the tops of window reveals to reduce staining to the soffit and to reduce the amount of water reaching the windows. Cills are usually formed in metal sheet that throws water clear of the wall beneath, while metal copings are usually inclined in order to drain water onto the roof or gutter behind rather than down the face of the building.

The colour of concrete is influenced mainly by the choice of cement, with fair faced visible concrete walls using either grey or white cement bases to produce the concrete colours associated with each. The physical properties of these two cement types is very similar, with grey being associated with architectural concrete finishes and usually provides a consistent appearance, when pouring methods and conditions remain consistent during construction of the façade. The tone of grey will vary with the cement/water ratio, the porosity of the shuttering, vibration conditions, formwork stripping time and weather conditions. White cement is much more tolerant of variations in methods and site conditions in providing a consistent white colour.

The most common finishes for concrete walls cast in situ are either an as-cast finish or a washed finish. Other finishes are discussed in the section on precast panels: acid etching, sand blasting, tooling and polishing, though these additional finishes can be used on in situ cast concrete.

In as-cast finishes, the colour variations result not usually from the cement colour, but from the marbling effect of fine particles of sand becoming unevenly distributed during vibration when the concrete is poured in place. Smooth concrete is typically self-coloured in large areas of façade, though pigments are giving ever improved results. Smooth and visually consistent natural finishes are achieved largely by the accuracy of mixed proportions including water.

← Isometric view of assembly

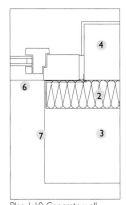

Plan 1:10. Concrete wall.
Insulation set within wall

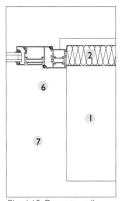

Plan 1:10. Concrete wall.
Insulation set on internal face

Section 1:10. Loadbearing concrete wall.
Insulation set within wall.

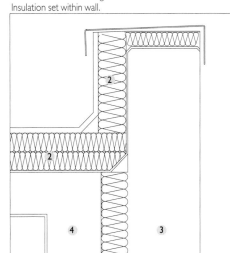

Tod's, Tokyo. Architect: Toyo Ito

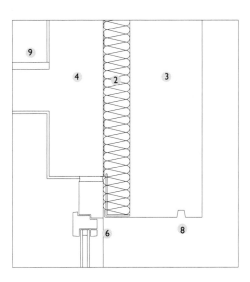

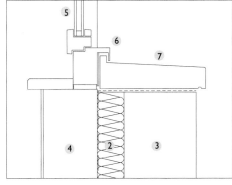

Section 1:50. In situ cast concrete wall cast as two leaves with rigid closed cell insulation between (above) and as single wall with insulation set on internal face (below).

Textured finishes can be formed with specially formed shuttering boards or with an additional lining sheet containing the texture pattern. Polystyrene or synthetic rubber sheet are commonly used. Recesses joints are usually introduced between the formwork boards to avoid uneven and blurred lines at the junction between boards. Washed finishes are formed by applying a 'deactivator' to the external face of the concrete, either to the face of the formwork before casting or to the concrete surface when the formwork has been removed. The deactivator is used to slow down or stop hydration of the cement, applied by brush or spray. The concrete is washed to revealing the texture below.

Details
1. Single concrete wall
2. Thermal insulation
3. Outer leaf
4. Inner leaf
5. Single/double glazed

unit to suit application
6. Window
7. Metal/concrete cill
8. Drip
9. Internal floor level
10. External level

cast in situ loadbearing walls

façades technical review

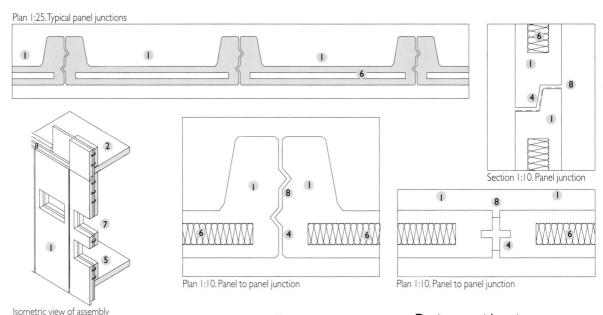

Plan 1:25. Typical panel junctions

Section 1:10. Panel junction

Plan 1:10. Panel to panel junction

Isometric view of assembly

Plan 1:10. Panel to panel junction

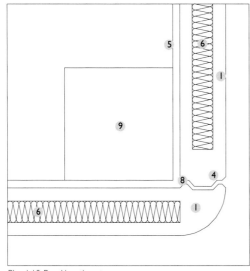

Plan 1:10. Panel junction at corner

Plan 1:10. Panel junction at corner

Details

1. Precast concrete panel
2. Concrete floor
3. Steel dowel/ Steel angle
4. Synthetic rubber baffle
5. Dry lining
6. Rigid thermal insulation
7. Window unit
8. Synthetic rubber seal
9. Structural column

Sandblasting and tooling are common on small cladding panels. Sandblasting is done with iron filings rather than sand particles. The blasting slightly erodes the face of the concrete, either back to the surface sand grains or more deeply to the coarse aggregate beneath, resulting in a matt finish. Localised work can be done with stencils. Tooled concrete is a method of texturing concrete with chisels or picks to make grooves or continuous textures. The textures usually stop short of corners of walls to give a crisp edge.

Design considerations

While in situ cast walls are loadbearing, precast walls can be used either as panels 'stitched' together to form a loadbearing wall, or as cladding panels. Loadbearing types have storey height panels stacked together which are made integral with the floor slabs. Junctions are usually pin jointed, with structural stability provided by other elements such as service cores elsewhere in the building. Loadbearing spandrel panels can also be formed as structural beams between precast columns, allowing full length glazing to be used, rather than the separate openings associated with full height precast panels. Non-loadbearing cladding panels typically span from floor to floor, with some panels, mainly sandwich panel types, supported directly on the floor slabs, while others are set forward of the slabs, fixed back to the floor structure with brackets made typically from stainless steel or reinforced concrete. The type of fixing used is very much dependent on the spatial requirements within the building and whether or not concrete nibs can be made visible or be concealed within the internal finishes.

Due to their self weight, panels are usually supported at their base on the floor slabs and are restrained at the top of the panel with mechanical fixings. Panels are usually a maximum of around 3600mm wide to suit road transportation, and a maximum weight of around 10 tonnes to suit regular site cranes. As with in situ cast concrete walls, the thermal insulation can be set either on the inside face of the panels or within a diaphragm wall construction. Insulation is set on the outside

Laboratory Building, Utrecht. Architect: UN Studio

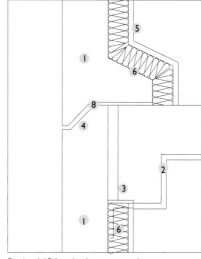

Section 1:10. Junction between panels.
Panels insulated on inside face.

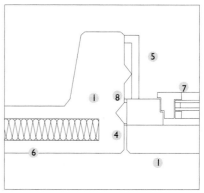

Plan 1:10. Panel-to-panel junction and window jamb

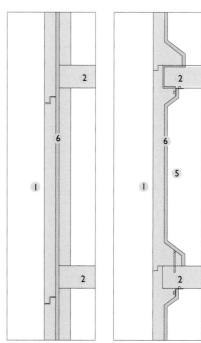

Sections 1:25. Typical precast concrete walls:
Internally insulated panels (left),
insulated on inside face (right)

of the wall where the panel forms a backing wall to a different material fixed to the face of the precast panel.

Panels are manufactured in flat moulds, with the finished face at the bottom of the mould when the concrete finish is required to be visible, or with the finished face on the top of the mould where another material is applied such as ceramic tiles, or where metal fixings for a masonry finish are cast into the face of the panel. Where a concrete finish is formed in the bottom of the panel, textured finishes are formed within the mould, usually by a synthetic rubber mat or polystyrene.

Design solutions

Joints between panels are similar for both loadbearing and cladding panel types. The methods used are either 'open' or 'closed' joints. Open joints have an outer narrow but open joint that admits a relatively small amount of rainwater which is drained down an inner chamber and back to the outside at the base of the panel through a stepped horizontal joint. This internally drained and pressure equalised system is similar in concept to that used in unitised curtain walling. In closed joints the outer face is sealed with a wet applied silicone or polysulphide sealant in a similar way to the sealing of joints between bolt fixed glazed panels. Joint widths both vertically and horizontally for both open and closed joints vary from 10–25mm increasing with panel width up to a maximum of around 6000mm.

In vertical open joints, the inner chamber between panels is closed with a synthetic rubber strip which provides a primary seal. The interior face of both vertical and horizontal joints is closed with an air seal formed with either an extruded synthetic rubber gasket or a wet-applied sealant. Loadbearing panels are sealed with a cement-based grout. Closed joints are mostly used in loadbearing panel construction where panels are mechanically fixed together.

The most common finishes in precast panels are acid etched, polished, sand blasted and tooled finishes. The last two techniques are discussed in the next section on small precast panels but these techniques can be applied equally here. Polished finishes are formed by an abrasive grinding wheel lubricated with water that removes up to 2mm of the material with a single pass of the grinder to a honed or fully polished finish. This exposes the colour of the aggregate but the surface does not shine naturally. Varnishes can be applied to achieve this stone-like appearance.

Acid etched finishes are well suited to precast panels since the amount of acid applied can be more carefully controlled in the factory than can be achieved on site. The outer face of the panel is treated with hydrochloric acid to reveal the concrete texture beneath, which is then rinsed off, having the effect of revealing the concrete texture immediately beneath. Acid etching attacks limestone aggregates, and sometimes more quickly than it does the cement, while silica-based aggregate remains. The surface texture achieved varies with the fine aggregate used, being more granulated in the case of silica and less coloured in the case of limestone.

Kashiwanoha-Campus Station, Japan.
Architect: Makoto Sei Watanabe/Architects' Office

Plan 1:10. Window junctions and corners. →
GRC panels with open joints

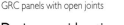

Section 1:25. Typical precast concrete panel types

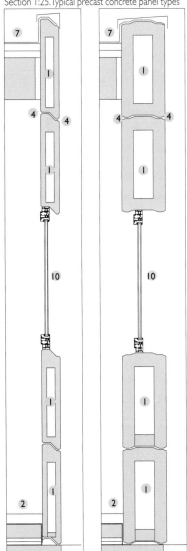

Design considerations

Small precast concrete panels have become increasingly popular over the past 10 years partly as a result of the greater sense of visual variety possible with a reduced unit size. Where storey height panels suit larger scale projects, smaller self-supporting and interlocking panels are stacked together in the manner of composite metal panels. In addition, individually supported rainscreen panels use the language of stone or metal panel façades.

Self-supporting panels have an inner core of thermal insulation with a finished concrete face on each visible side of the panel. Individually supported rainscreen panels are fixed directly to an insulated backing wall, with open joints that follow rainscreen principles. Interlocking panels can be stacked to a single storey height of around 10 metres and at every floor level in buildings with more than one storey. Panels at ground floor level are set on a beam edge to a concrete floor or similar foundation beam. Panels are stacked with continuous vertical joints and are restrained by columns. The need to support panels at joints results in their being wide in order to optimise the distance between columns which is determined by the required structural grid. The long panels compensate in size by being low in height in order to reduce their weight that can be lifted by a smaller site crane, typically with a lifting capacity of 4 to 6 tonnes.

Since panels have concrete on all sides, both horizontal joints and vertical joints usually have a limited thermal bridge which can lead to pattern staining as a result of dif-ferent rates of thermal transmittance in the material, in addition to the increased risk of condensation occurring on the internal face. The thermal bridge can be avoided by the use of metal connections between two skins of concrete in place of a full concrete block, but this makes it more difficult to stack blocks and to maintain the economy of the system. Self-supporting stacked panels fabricated in thicknesses of 75–100mm can also form part of a complete cavity wall construction of 200–300mm thickness. The inner wall can vary widely in its construction from concrete block to light gauge metal stud wall with an outer waterproof facing. The cavity between concrete panels and backing wall is 50–75mm, ventilated at the top and bottom of the wall.

Individually supported panels can provide narrower joints than those possible in full height panels, together with the possibility of a non-rectilinear arrangement of joints. Fixing brackets are similar to those used for stone cladding, but are usually bigger to support the heavier panels. Where stone panel sizes are typically around 1500mm × 750mm or 1500mm × 1000mm, depending on stone type, precast panels can typically reach 1500mm × 3000mm. Panels are supported on stainless steel brackets which are either cast-in or are bolted to the structure. Slotted holes in the bracket provide adjustment vertically, horizontally and laterally. In common with stone cladding, individually supported concrete panels are supported on short lengths of stainless steel angle at each floor level in order to avoid the possibility of progressive collapse of cladding panels in the event of a single panel failing or slipping

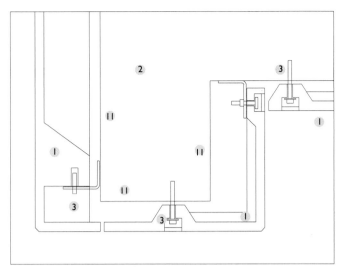

Section 1:10. Panel soffit junction. GRC panels with open joints

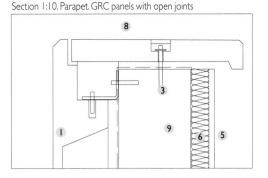

Section 1:10. Parapet. GRC panels with open joints

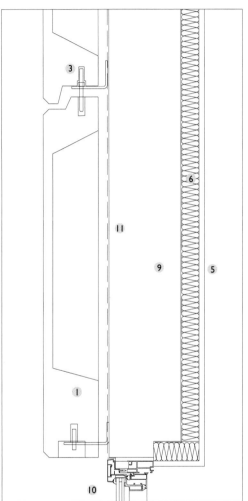

from its position. Panels at floor level are fixed directly to the slab, with fixings designed so that they can support the full load of the panels immediately above it in the event of fixings to panels above failing either partially or completely.

Design solutions

An advantage of small precast panels is that interfaces with openings, parapets and cills are relatively straightforward. The interfaces discussed here are for stacked panels. Those for individually supported panels are similar to those for stone cladding. Windows are fitted into openings relatively easily, since the stepped profile at the base of the panel provides a natural cill profile to the opening. The concrete facing to all sides of the panel provides weathertight edges on the jambs and at the head of the opening. Windows are set in a position which suits the profile of the precast panel, typically in the middle of the opening, but windows can also project forward of the opening with the use of metal flashings to seal the window at its perimeter.

The closing of parapets is provided by a metal flashing that covers the panel and any parapet wall that may be set behind the panels to close off the roof. The coping is sloped towards the roof to ensure that rainwater is not directed down the façade. A precast coping can also be used instead of aluminium, but this is a visually-based decision. An additional membrane is set under the metal or concrete coping to ensure a fully watertight seal.

Details

1. Precast concrete panel
2. Concrete floor
3. Stainless steel fixing
4. Synthetic rubber seal
5. Dry lining
6. Thermal insulation
7. Roof construction
8. Coping panel
9. Backing wall
10. Window
11. Waterproof membrane

The base of the walls are detailed in a similar way to other forms of loadbearing masonry. A continuous damp proof membrane (DPM) extends up from the outside of the structure beneath and forms a damp proof course (DPC) which is positioned so that it extends at least 150mm above external ground level. The DPC is positioned so that the lowest row of panels at ground level appears to sit on the ground with its bottom edge either level, or slightly above the adjacent ground level or pavement. This avoids the need for a 150–200mm waterproofed plinth at the base of the wall.

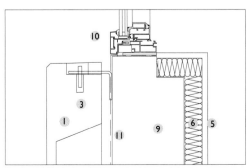

Section 1:10. Window. GRC panels with open joints

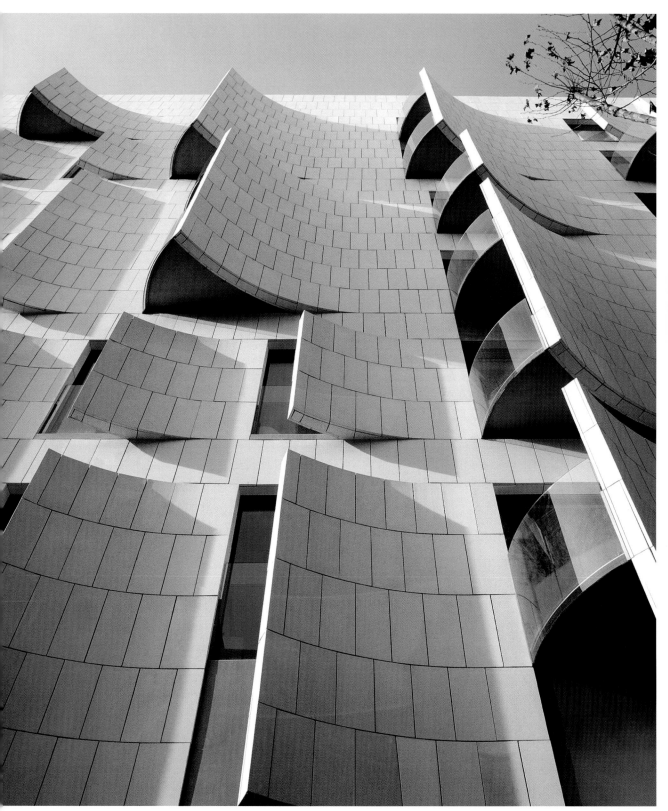

There has been a renewal of interest in loadbearing masonry construction as an alternative to cavity wall construction, with external walls supporting floors and roof. With this method, thermal insulation is set either on the inside face of a single massive wall or within the wall where a diaphragm wall is used. The Pfanner House in Chicago by Zoka Zola uses the potential of brick as a cladding material that uses the same material as others in the street but does not follow the language of traditional loadbearing construction. Terracotta rainscreens have become very economic in recent years, with more systems having interlocking terracotta panels that provides a continuous surface without highly visible joints. In the EMI Building in Paris by Renzo Piano the material no longer imitates the appearance of brickwork or wall tiling associated with earlier examples. Stone cladding uses fixings and carrier systems which are ever-higher performing, allowing a more technically ambitious use of stone, as seen in the Hotel Omm in Barcelona by Juli Capella.

04_

masonry

Photographs. Top (left to right): Selwyn College, Cambridge, England. Architect: Porphyrios Associates; Pfanner House, Chicago, USA. Architect: Zoka Zola; EMI Building, Paris, France. Architect: Renzo Piano Building Workshop. Opposite page: Hotel Omm, Barcelona, Spain. Architect: Juli Capella

Selwyn College, Cambridge, England. Architect: Porphyrios Associates

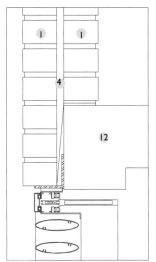

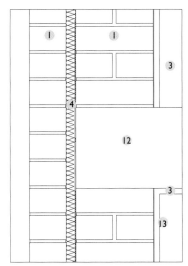

Sections 1:10. Insulated diaphragm walls

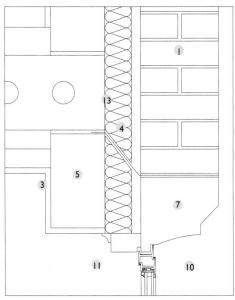

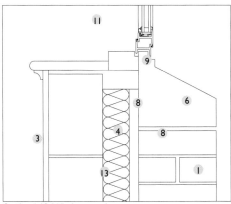

Section 1:10. Window openings

Details

1. Loadbearing brick wall
2. Loadbearing block wall
3. Internal finish or dry lining
4. Thermal insulation
5. Lintel, precast concrete shown
6. Cill, precast concrete shown
7. Brick arch
8. Damp proof course (DPC)
9. Weather bar
10. Seal
11. Window, timber framed shown
12. Floor slab
13. Vapour barrier
14. Render
15. Coping

In parapets, the coping piece has a damp proof course (DPC) set beneath it to avoid rainwater being absorbed into the wall beneath. The DPC is continuous with the roof waterproofing layer. In common with copings in other materials, the top is sloped inwards to drain water towards the roof rather than down the façade where it would cause staining. The coping usually projects beyond the face of the wall on the roof side to throw water clear.

Design considerations

Loadbearing masonry walls are most commonly made from brick or concrete block. In continental Europe, terracotta blocks are more common, but are usually rendered on their external face, both to enhance their appearance and for its traditional role as a weather tight outer layer. Concrete blocks are similarly protected by render. Only brickwork is usually fully exposed, relying on the depth of wall to avoid the ingress of rainwater.

In brick construction, it is assumed that a 315mm thick wall (1½ bricks) is the minimum depth sufficient to resist rainwater penetration in temperate climates. This is dependent upon brick density and the mortar used. With brick, thermal insulation is set on the inside face to allow the material to be visible on the outside, but with concrete block, the insulation can be set on the outside with an external layer of render to provide the weatherproof skin. An alternative solution is to set thermal insulation within the wall, creating a loadbearing diaphragm wall where the brick or block can be seen on both sides of the wall, and also allows the internal face of the wall to be used for night time cooling within the building. Two skins of brick, typically 215mm to 315mm thick, are set apart, joined by fin walls set perpendicular to the main walls. Concrete block walls are made from skins 200mm to 300mm thick. The position of the insulation within the walls, or on the internal face of the wall, allows a straightforward continuity with the thermal insulation provided by windows within openings.

An essential benefit of using loadbearing masonry walls is their ability to avoid the need

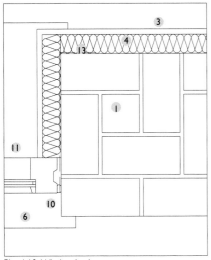

Plan 1:10. Window jamb

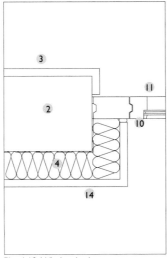

Plan 1:10. Window jamb

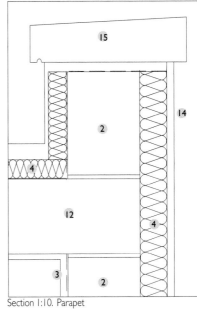

Section 1:10. Parapet

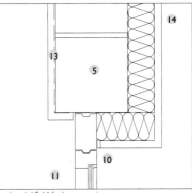

Section 1:10. Window openings

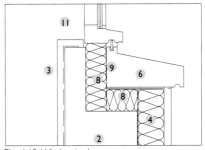

Plan 1:10. Window jamb

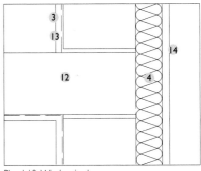

Plan 1:10. Window jamb

for visible movement joints through the use of flexible mortar, typically lime mortar. This traditional material has lower strength than mortars used in contemporary cavity wall construction but has greater flexibility, allowing it to move more freely without cracking. This reduces, or can even avoid the need for, movement joints which are introduced to avoid cracking in masonry walls. Movement joints in walls where cement-based mortars are used are set typically at 6.0–8.0 metres depending on the required strength and size of wall. In lime mortars the strength of mortars is varied by altering the proportion of cement and lime which are used to bind the mortar together. Generally speaking, increasing the proportion of cement will increase its strength, while increasing that of lime increases its flexibility, with mortar mixes having different proportions of strength and flexibility. In addition, the comparatively low water permeability of lime gives it greater resistance to rain penetration than mortar mixes with a high proportion of cement. Lime has the effect of making mortars increasingly light in colour with its increased proportion in the mix. However, mortar colour can be modified by adding pigments to the mix. Where stone is used on the outer face of the loadbearing wall, typically facing a brick wall behind, the mortar has crushed stone added in place of sand in order to give mortar the texture and some of the appearance of the stone itself.

Design solutions

Openings in loadbearing masonry walls have the ability to reveal the thickness of the wall, giving it a massive appearance. Cills to openings are formed from either the same material if stone is used for the wall or, more commonly, precast concrete. Sometimes the timber or metal cill that forms part of the window is used to form the cill where visual criteria permits its use. Cills are sloped with a projecting edge that throws the rainwater clear of the wall beneath. A throating is also used to avoid water running back to the external face of the wall from the underside of the projecting cill. Where stone is used, the material must be sufficiently impervious or alternatively have sufficient slope to allow water to run off quickly. Where softer stones are used, such as sandstones and limestones, the material must be sufficiently dense and durable to avoid staining occurring due to water absorption Cills are usually made as single pieces to avoid joints being formed which are less impervious than the cill material. A DPC is set under the cill to ensure that rainwater penetrating the outer cill drains away any water that soaks through it, particularly at the joints. The heads of openings in loadbearing masonry walls are supported by lintels or arches. In traditional brick construction, a flat or curved arch is used to support the brickwork above. In concrete block construction, a reinforced concrete lintel is used, which spans the complete width of the wall, while in stone a thin arch is used on the outer face of the wall, often with a more rudimentary brick arch or concrete lintel behind it, concealed by the window frame.

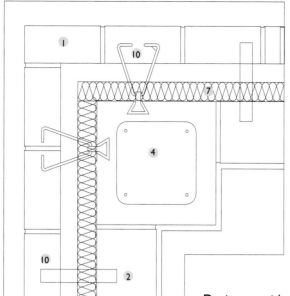

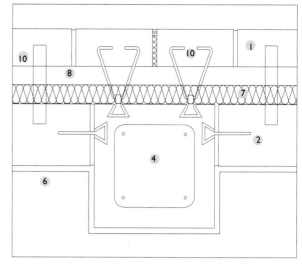

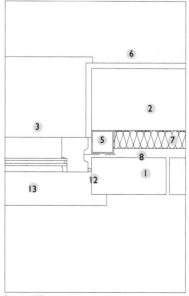

Plan 1:10. Corner conditions

Plan 1:10. Typical window jamb

Design considerations

Where loadbearing brick walls use the overall wall thickness to stop the passage of rainwater from outside to inside, cavity walls use two skins of masonry separated by a ventilated air gap, where only the outer skin is ever saturated with water. The inner skin is usually formed in concrete block or timber studwork, with thermal insulation usually set on the external face of the inner skin.

Historically, inner and outer skins were tied together with floor slabs to form diaphragm walls, but their use is reduced with the concern over the thermal bridge created by linking the two skins of brick. Current practice uses the outer skin as cladding to a drained and ventilated void behind, with an inner skin that is waterproofed with a high level of thermal insulation. The cavity is vented top and bottom to ensure the free passage of air through the cavity. This allows the cavity to remain dry as well as assisting in drying the outer skin of brick, which can become fully saturated in a rainstorm. The cavity is bridged only by openings for windows and doors.

The outer brick skin is usually only 100mm thick (one brick width) with both skins being supported either at ground level, at intermediary floor levels and at the roof. The inner skin is built off each floor slab and is restrained at the head by the floor slab or roof structure above. Taller buildings have the inner skin built directly onto floor slabs in the same way, but the outer skin is supported at each floor level on a continuous stainless steel angle, bolted back to the floor slab. A damp proof course (DPC) is set on top of the steel angle to drain the cavity. Weep holes (vertical slots)

are formed in the vertical joints immediately above the steel angle in order to allow water in the cavity to drain out. In addition to being restrained at floor slabs, the outer skin is also tied at intermediary points back to the inner skin with stainless steel ties. These are set typically at 450mm horizontal centres and 900mm vertical centres. Vertical movement joints are provided at around 7500mm centres, or else are avoided altogether in the construction by keeping lengths of wall within these dimensions.

Design solutions

When an opening is formed, the cavity is closed by a lintel to support the inner and outer skins at the top of the opening, and a cill piece at the bottom of the opening. The sides are closed by either returning one of the two skins to meet the other skin, or by setting an insulated cavity closer into the gap, usually made as an aluminium extrusion filled with thermal insulation. Because the downward passage of water inside the cavity is blocked by the lintel at the head of the opening, a cavity tray formed from bituminous felt is set above the lintel to drain water out of the cavity. Water is drained at the bottom of the tray through weep holes in the vertical joints immediately above the DPC. The ends of the DPC are tucked down into a vertical DPC set into the jambs (sides) of the opening which is in turn linked to a DPC set under the cill to form a complete watertight seal to the opening which is drained to the outside. A similar principle of cavity tray is used to drain water at roof level and at ground level. In addition, a DPC is used at ground level to avoid water

Pfanner House, Chicago, USA. Architect: Zoka Zola

being drawn up into the wall construction to the inside face of the wall within the building. DPCs are also used beneath parapets and copings as well as at the junction of wall and pitched roof.

The position of the DPC at ground floor level is dependent upon the difference in height between ground floor level in the building and the adjacent external level. The DPC in the outer skin is set at around 150mm above external ground level. The DPC for the internal skin is set at the same level if the step up from outside to inside is around 150mm. If the difference between outside and inside levels is around 300mm then the DPC is stepped up from outer skin to inner skin in the same place but a separate DPC is added to the inner skin at the same level as the bottom of the cavity tray.

While there are many variations for eaves junctions, the top of the wall maintains a consistent principle of closing the cavity at the top with a brick or block that either allows the load from the roof structure to be supported on the inner skin or, alternatively, the roof structure may be supported on a column set into the inner skin of the wall or on blockwork piers, also forming part of the inner skin. The closing of the cavity wall at the top allows for continuity of thermal insulation from cavity wall to roof structure while allowing the roof construction to be ventilated where required, and the top of the cavity in the wall to be ventilated. A DPC is set to ensure continuity of waterproofing.

Details
1. Outer masonry wall
2. Inner masonry wall
3. Timber framed window
4. Structural column
5. Cavity closer
6. Internal finish or dry lining
7. Thermal insulation
8. Air cavity
9. Inner precast concrete lintel
10. Cavity tie
11. Steel angle
12. Seal
13. Cill, brick shown
14. Damp proof course (DPC)

Parapets are closed at the top by a coping, usually in reinforced concrete or stone. A DPC is set beneath the coping to stop the passage of water downwards. Below this, rainwater can enter the cavity from both inner and outer skins and this is prevented by extending the waterproof layer from the roof up the side of the inner skin up to coping level. Thermal insulation is usually continued up the inside of the cavity wall as well as up the external face of the inner skin to avoid a thermal bridge through the inner skin.

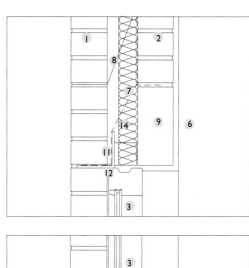

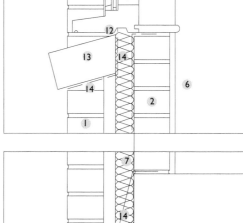

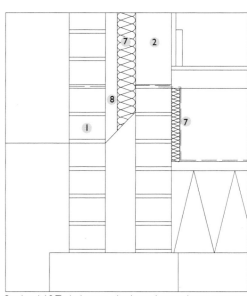

Section 1:10. Typical connection/restraint to primary structure

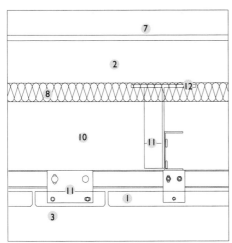

Plan 1:10. Typical stone carrier system made from extruded aluminium sections

Details

1. Stone panel
2. Backing wall
3. Stainless steel fixings
4. Timber framed window
5. Stone cill
6. Timber inner cill
7. Internal finish or dry lining
8. Thermal insulation
9. Stone coping
10. Air cavity
11. Carrier system
12. Waterproofing layer
13. Seal

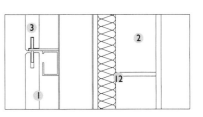

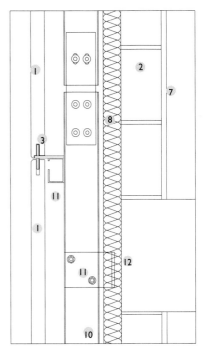

Section 1:10. Typical stone carrier system

Museum, Almira, Spain. Architect: Paredes Pedrosa

In the photograph, the stone cladding at the Museum by Paredes Pedrosa uses the material as a cladding to a façade conceived around a reinforced concrete structure. The mixture of large stone panels with long narrow panels gives a visual drama not usually associated with stone cladding. The expression of stone as a 'wrap' to a backing wall in a different material and unusual form, is set to continue.

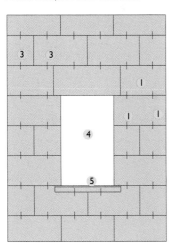

Section 1:50. Typical stone carrier system with typical fixing positions shown

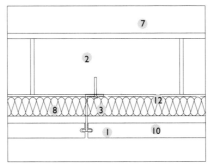

Plan 1:10. Stone supported on individual fixings

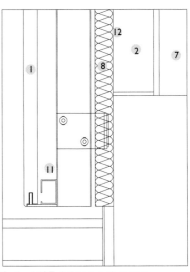

Section 1:10. Stone supported on carrier system

Design considerations

In this cladding method, stone panels are fixed back either directly to a backing wall or to a metal carrier frame with a separate backing wall behind. The use of stone for cladding requires considerable planning, from setting the range of colours, and textures of the material, to establishing the physical properties of the actual stone, to a structural design that establishes or confirms panel dimensions and suitable fixing methods. The physical properties of the stone may be available from the quarry at an early stage, but sometimes the testing is done during the early procurement stage to ensure that the material meets the requirements of particular building code. The thickness of stone required for a façade is usually established by structural calculation. Flexural strength, also called the modulus of rupture, is usually the most significant structural consideration in establishing panel size. Codes of practice often set out minimum thickness for various panel sizes in different sizes, but this is only a general guide and calculation is usually undertaken for specific façade applications. Since the material may not already be cut from the quarry at the time of its selection, stone façades can involve longer procurement times than for other façade systems.

Stainless steel is used for stone fixings because of its resistance to corrosion combined with high strength and rigidity. The fixings have a three way adjustment vertically, horizontally and laterally in order to align the stone panels accurately. The type of fixing used varies with the thickness and stone type used. Fixings are usually set at the top and bottom of the panel, with the bottom fixings being loadbearing and the fixings at the top of the panel being restraints. Side fixings are sometimes used depending on the weight and strength of the panel.

Design solutions

Fixings used to support stones that clad soffits are suspended from bolts or hangers which slide into anchorages cast into the supporting structure. Joints are either of 'open' or 'closed' type. Closed joints sealed with mortar or sealant are used where the cladding is supported at each floor level on stainless steel angles with jointed stones. With open jointed stones, each panel is individually supported in a rainscreen construction, where rainwater passing through the joints is drained away down either the back of the stones or down the face of the backing wall, which is typically insulated.

The choice of joint type is partly visual and partly to ensure adequate ventilation to the cavity allowing stone to dry properly. Closed joints allow the stone cladding to perform in a similar way to a cavity wall, with ventilation provided top and bottom to dry the void behind the stone. Closed joints in sandstones and limestones are usually filled with sand/cement mortar or sand/cement/lime mortar. Granites and slates typically are proprietary sealants such as two part polysulphide. Mortar used for pointing is made frost resistant when used in temperate climates, and of similar strength to the joining mortar, which is the structural mortar behind. The maximum width of mortar filled joints is around 12mm, but sealant filled joints can exceed this, subject to visual requirements. Joint widths are partly a function of the cutting tolerance of the stone, which can vary along its length by up to 2mm, depending on stone panel size and the cutting machine used. Joint widths of 4m are common, but this can rise to around 12mm when required for visual reasons.

Movement joints are set both horizontally and vertically to accommodate movements in the building structure. Horizontal movement joints are used to deal mainly with structural deflections in floor slabs, and are usually provided at floor level, where the stone cladding is supported from either short lengths of stainless steel angle, or a continuous steel angle. The movement joint is set immediately below the stainless steel angle, where vertical deflection will occur. Horizontal movement joints can be set at intervals of two storeys if a carrier frame is used that will span the full height. The joint width is usually around 20mm wide. The joint can be formed as open or closed to suit the jointing method.

Vertical movement joints are provided in façades where they coincide with the building structure and are set immediately forward of these movement joints. The distance between joints is typically at around 6 metres in a continuous run of stone cladding with closed joints. The joint width corresponds to the expected movement in the cladding, but where sealed joints are used, the joint width is dependent on the amount of movement that the sealant is required to accommodate.

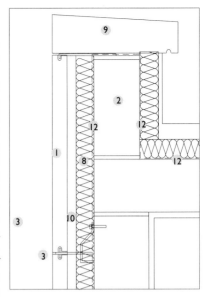

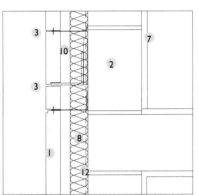

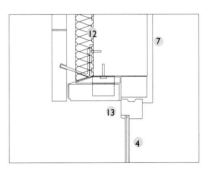

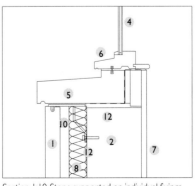

Section 1:10. Stone supported on individual fixings

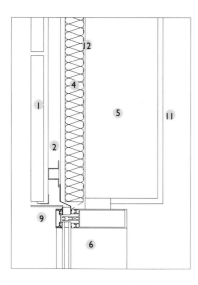

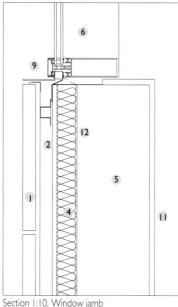

Section 1:10. Window jamb

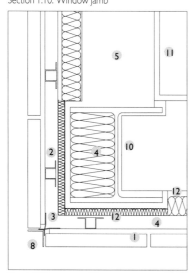

Plan 1:10. Corner condition

Design considerations

Terracotta rainscreens have developed from prototypes to full proprietary systems within the last 15 years. Over that time the sizes of terracotta panels have increased and fixing systems have developed. Louvres are formed from hollow terracotta sections reinforced internally with aluminium sections to form panels of screens that can match with adjacent areas of terracotta cladding. Terracotta is fixed either on rails, into aluminium or stainless steel panels, is supported on individual brackets in the manner of masonry cladding. Vertically-set or horizontally-set rails are used to suit a range of joint arrangements that imitate traditional masonry bonds, or alternatively can be fixed in a stack bonded arrangement. Recently developed systems have interlocking panels to provide visually crisp joints, and double wall sections to provide long spanning panels. The range of glazed finishes has developed considerably in the past few years to give a very wide range of textures and colour mixes derived from contemporary pottery. Terracotta is made from natural clay that is first extruded and then fired in a kiln. The use of extrusion dies allows the manufacture of terracotta panels to be flexible from project to project. As with aluminium framed curtain walling, the die creates different heights and depths of block while maintaining a hollow interior to keep the material relatively light and easy to handle, allowing it to be made in long pieces if required.

Design solutions

Because terracotta panels have two extruded edges and two cut edges, panels are arranged so as to avoid a cut edge being revealed at a corner. This is because the surface finish and colour of the end face will not match that of the front face. The ends of panels are usually concealed with aluminium trims, sometimes at the corners but typically around window openings. Alternatively, special corner shapes can be formed by hand to match the standard extruded tiles, made by a pressing method, usually with a maximum length of 150mm on one leg and 300mm on the other. Large corner pieces are made by hand by joining two sections together, but these currently produce less reliable results that can lack a straight and crisp edge. In addition, manufacturers often provide extruded cill sections for parapets and window sec-

tions to suit wall constructions of 300mm to 500mm wide. Fired terracotta is either left in its natural colour or is glazed. A glazed finish can give the material more visual sparkle by making the surface more reflective, which also provides better protection from surface staining. However, water absorption of regular terracotta panels is between 3 per cent and 6 per cent, with a density of around 2000kg/m3, making the use of glazes not essential for excluding rainwater but important more for visual reasons.

Panels are fixed to support rails which are set either vertically or horizontally, made from aluminium for their ability to be formed precisely as extrusions for ease of fixing. Vertical rails are well suited to 'stack bonded' terracotta, where joints form a rectilinear grid of continuous vertical and horizontal joints. Horizontal rails are suited to staggered bonds of panels that imitate the stretcher bond used in traditional wall construction where vertical joints are not continuous, at least twice as many vertical rails are needed as those for a stack bond arrangement. Since horizontal joints are continuous, horizontal rails are used to fix courses of terracotta. Joint widths vary from 2mm to around 10mm, depending on the size of panel and type of fixing system chosen. The largest panels are planks up to around 1500mm long x 600mm wide x 40mm thick, requiring a substantial aluminium support section behind the panels. The extrusions, set at the ends of each panel, sometimes project forward of the terracotta in order to provide sufficient rigidity. This gives the façade a characteristic appearance of vertical bays of panels, where only vertical backing supports are used, divided by the visible edge of the aluminium support. Corner pieces can be made in sizes of 250mm x 300mm high, which often do not match with the maximum height that can be manufactured for the planks, but this constraint will no doubt be overcome in the next few years. Thinner terracotta panels of 30mm thickness are used, in sizes with a maximum length of around 800mm and corresponding maximum height of 300mm. These thinner panels have maximum corner panels of 150mm on one leg and 300mm on the other leg. The minimum sizes that can be accommodated with the vertical rail system are terracotta panels around 200mm long x 200mm high, with a thickness of 30–40mm.

EMI Building, Paris, France. Architect: Renzo Piano Building Workshop

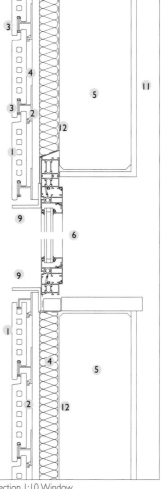

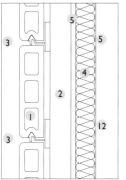

Section 1:10. Joint

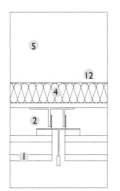

Plan 1:10. Joint

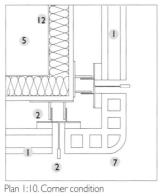

Plan 1:10. Corner condition

Section 1:10. Window

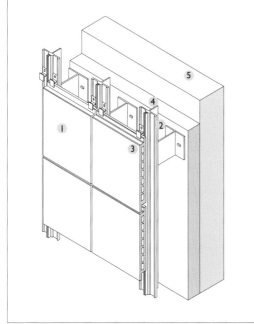

Isometric view of wall assembly

Details

1. Terracotta rainscreen
2. Aluminium carrier frame
3. Fixing clip
4. Thermal insulation
5. Backing wall
6. Window, aluminium shown
7. Corner panel
8. Metal corner trim
9. Metal window trim
10. Structural column
11. Internal finish or dry lining
12. Waterproof layer

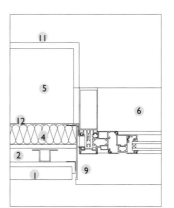

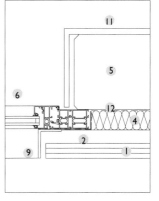

Plan 1:10. Window

Polycarbonate, acrylic and GRP (glass reinforced polyester) are finding more ambitious applications in façades from interlocking cladding panels, to rainscreen panels, to complete envelope shells. GRP has been used as an outer waterproofing layer to plywood panels in the M7 House in Chile by UR01.ORG, developed for use in emergency and low cost housing though its use in more mainstream construction will surely follow. Twin wall polycarbonate sheet can be used with glass in translucent, highly insulated walls that provide well lit spaces, as in the project in Korea by Florian Beigel and ARU. Translucent plastic panels have been formed into lightweight folding and lifting panels in the Paper Museum by Shigeru Ban where the panels are well suited to use as moving façade elements. Plastic rainscreen panels provide the opportunity for curved transparent panels to be used where glass would be too expensive and would be difficult to manufacture, particularly for point fixed solutions such as the Art Museum in Graz by Spacelab Cook-Fournier.

05_
plastic

façades technical review

Photographs. Top (left to right): M7 House, Punta de Gallo, Chile. Architect: UR01.ORG; Mixed Use Project, South Korea.
Architect: Florian Beigel; Art Museum, Graz, Austria. Architect: Spacelab Cook-Fournier.
Opposite page: Publishing House, Paju Bookcity, Seoul, Korea. Architect: Florian Beigel with Architecture Research Unit, London

61

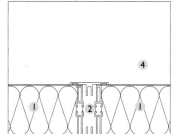

Plan 1:10. Panel-to-panel

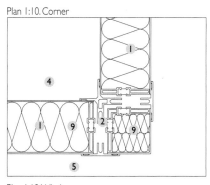

Plan 1:10. Corner

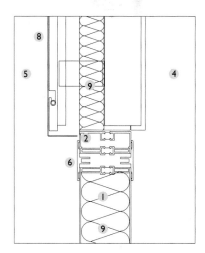

Section 1:10. Junctions at adjacent wall types

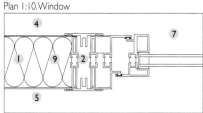

Section 1:10. Panel-to-panel

Plan 1:10. Window

Design considerations

Plastics are resinous, polymer-based materials, used for both sealed cladding and rainscreens. The materials used are principally glass reinforced polyester (GRP), polycarbonate and UPVC. This section discusses the use of GRP in sealed cladding panels which is the most common material used. GRP is a composite material made from thermosetting polyester resins (which set hard and do not melt when re-heated) that are mixed with glass fibre mat. This composite material has high tensile, shear and compressive strength combined with lightness and resistance to corrosion. However, like aluminium it deflects considerably under high loads and requires stiffening, but is more rigid than other plastics. GRP is not combustible and can reach one hour fire resistance in some cladding applications. GRP panels are formed by laying glass fibre cloth into a mould and coating it with resin and catalyst, or alternatively spraying a mixture of glass fibre and resin into a mould. The face of the mould is coated with a releasing agent to allow the GRP to be removed when it has set hard.

An advantage of GRP panels is their lightness in weight, combined with being manufactured by moulding, allowing them to be made in large panel sizes, up to 6000mm x 1500mm. Panel thicknesses are usually 70-75mm to provide structural stability and thermal insulation. Panels are made from two moulded GRP skins which are bonded either side of the rigid insulation. In common with metal composite panels, GRP panels have undergone much development in the use of adhesives to avoid delamination between the outer skins and the insulation core. GRP cladding panels can be made either as separate panels glazed into an aluminium pressure plate system (in a similar way to glass) with a secondary supporting structure behind, or alternatively by setting thermally broken aluminium extrusions within the depth of the panels. That allows them to be fixed together in the manner of composite metal panels. Panels are also stiffened internally with aluminium I-sections or T-sections where large scale panels are used.

Design solutions

The translucent panels have internal aluminium framing within the panel forming a visible grid, resembling traditional Japanese Shoji screens. These internal ribs are typically set out on a grid of between around 300mm x 300mm to 300mm x 600mm centres. The void between the two skins of the panel can be filled with translucent insulation quilt to increase thermal insulation, while still allowing a diffused light to pass through the panel. Light transmission without additional thermal insulation is typically around 15 per cent, with a U-value of 1.5W/m2 °C, similar to an argon filled double glazed unit, and a shading factor of 20 per cent, which provides a high level of shading for a glass-based wall. Windows can be glazed into the panels, giving the possibility of a rich mix of windows, doors and translucent panels without the need for complex framing. Window frames can form part of the T-section extrusion around a window. Integrating the window frame into the extrusion that supports the GRP panels avoids the risk of leaks associated with single silicone-

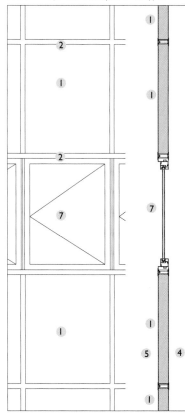

Elevation and section 1:25. Typical arrangement of panels with opening light

Section 1:10. Panel-to-panel

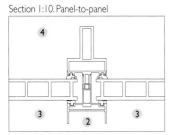

Section 1:10. Panel-to-panel

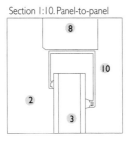

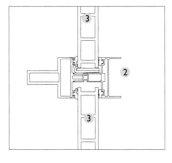

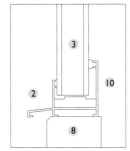

Paper Museum, Shizuoka, Japan. Architect: Shigeru Ban

sealed butt joints when a separate window frame and panel frame are fixed together. The integrated window frame allows water to be drained from the frame. GRP panels can be glazed into large structural openings, from floor to ceiling for example, or can form a complete glazed wall, restrained by a secondary steel frame. When glazed into an opening, the edge T-section aluminium profiles are sealed against the adjacent concrete floor slab with silicone, at both top and bottom. When fixed to a secondary support frame, panels are supported at each floor level on metal brackets in either aluminium, mild steel (if internal) or stainless steel (if exposed to the weather). Cills and copings are formed with the methods described in the section on metal composite panels.

Where twin wall polycarbonate is used in conjunction with other plastic-based panels, the material is fixed with either conventional aluminium framing for windows or, alternatively, framing for stick glazing curtain walling. Some manufacturers provide extruded I-sections, similar to those used in GRP cladding, to clip the twin wall sheets to provide a completely lightweight system. This is a very economic form of cladding which can be screen printed to create visually dramatic translucent façades. As with profiled polycarbonate sheet, other standard components are not usually manufactured, and folded aluminium sections are used for drips and parapet copings instead of polycarbonate sections, which are as expensive to produce as new profiles.

Details

1. Translucent GRP cladding panel, insulated
2. Thermally broken extruded aluminium framing
3. Twin wall polycarbonate sheet
4. Inside
5. Outside
6. Profiled polycarbonate sheet
7. Window inserted into framing
8. Adjacent wall. Metal rainscreen shown
9. Thermal insulation
10. Extruded aluminium edge frame

Although plastic-based panels are usually made panels fabricated entirely in a factory and fixed together on site in an extruded aluminium glazing system, they can also be formed on site by fixing plastic-based sheet either side of metal framing supports. The cladding may be formed into panels or may be constructed as a continuous wall structure to give a continuous façade texture. The use of translucent insulation as an infill material that is not fully bonded to the supporting plastic skins provides considerable possibilities for innovation.

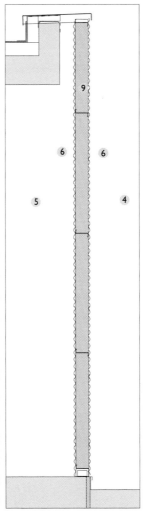

Section 1:25. Storey height panel

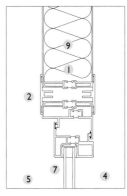

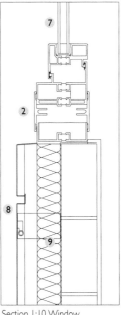

Section 1:10. Window

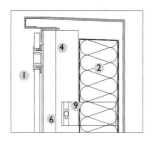

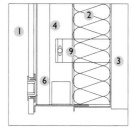

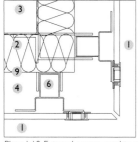

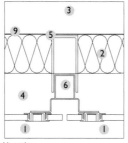

Plans 1:10. External corner, panel-to-panel junction

Details

1. Plastic rainscreen panel
2. Thermal insulation
3. Backing wall
4. Air gap
5. Internal finish
6. Extruded aluminium edge framing
7. Plastic or metal trim
8. Window
9. Waterproofing layer

Polycarbonate is generally a more expensive material than GRP, but GRP has one advantage over all the other plastic-based materials, in being moulded easily and economically. When used as rainscreen panels the material needs a top gel coat to provide durability. For moulded rainscreen panels it is possible to introduce some 3D modelling into the façade panels. GRP can be bonded to honeycomb panels formed in the same material to produce large panels with high fire resistance. The face of the panel can be screen printed to any design, with the use of photographic images being increasingly popular.

Design considerations

The main types of plastic-based rainscreen are flat panels, cassette panels, profiled sheet and overlapping tiles. They are used as either outer screens to glazed walls, typically as solar shading, or as rainscreen panels to an opaque wall. The materials used are either polycarbonate or glass reinforced polyester (GRP). Acrylic and UPVC, while softer than both these materials, are used for window frames and specially moulded elements. In addition, composites are used, made from thermosetting polymer resins mixed with cellulose fibres to provide sheet materials with high durability which fade little in sunlight. In common with rainscreens in other materials, panels or sheets are fixed with either visible point fixings, vertical/horizontal rails with partially concealed framing members, or partially interlocking panels where there is no view through the joints.

Polycarbonate is a thermoplastic (melts at high temperatures), which is used in cladding for its translucency and transparency, achieving up to around 90 per cent light transmission. The material is extruded or moulded (from polymer-formed granules) to form sheet materials that are flat or profiled. Polycarbonate has a tendency to yellow with age, which can be overcome with an acrylic coating. It is also used for its high strength and impact resistance, ductility and lightness in weight. However, because the material is combustible, its use in façades is limited. It is also less durable than glass, scratching easily which makes the surface dull with time, and has high thermal expansion, up to 20 per cent more than glass. Opaque flat sheet is fixed as

Isometric view of wall assembly

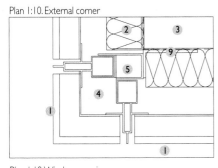

Plan 1:10. External corner

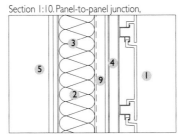

Plan 1:10. Internal corner

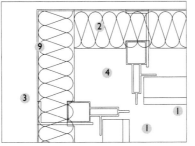

Section 1:10. Window opening

Plan 1:10. Window opening

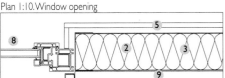

Section 1:10. Panel-to-panel junction,

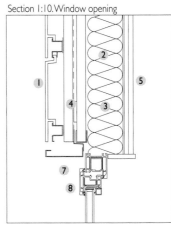

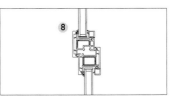

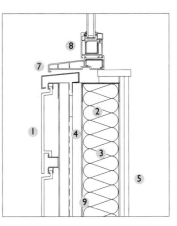

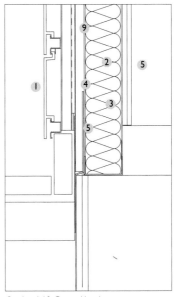

rainscreen cladding panels, made in a wide range of colours, Sheets are fixed either at their corners with an aluminium clamps on both sides, or with visible point fixings.

Single layer polycarbonate sheet sizes are around 2000mm × 3000mm and 2000mm × 6000mm, in thicknesses from around 3mm to 8mm. Profiled sheets are produced in lengths up to around 10 metres, around 1200mm wide, with thicknesses around 1mm. When opaque colours are used, rather than the translucent or clear types, hook-on fixings can be bonded to the rear face of the panel, secured to vertically-or horizontally-set rails without the fixings being visible.

Profiled sheets are fixed with simple point fixings and lapped on all sides, creating a shadow where they lap, which can be concealed by the support structure behind. Cill, drip and coping profiles are made from either extruded UPVC, GRP or extruded aluminium. Profiled sheet can be curved to a minimum radius of around 4000mm for a sheet of 50mm thickness. Profiled polycarbonate sheet is also made in a translucent white colour to provide a light transmission of around 45 per cent and in grey colours with light transmission of around 35 per cent.

Like flat sheet, multi-wall polycarbonate sheet can be used for rainscreens, where its main advantage is the ability to provide large, flat panels rather than its high level of thermal insulation. Thicknesses are from 4mm to 32mm in sheet sizes from 1000mm × 6000mm to 2000mm × 7000mm. The material can be screen printed or coated to provide a wide variety of colours on a large format sheet. As with flat sheet, the material

can be coated to give UV protection on one side or both sides to avoid yellowing. The sheet material is used in increasing wall thicknesses, from twin wall to five or six walls thick. Panels are fixed using the same methods as flat sheet, with thicker sheets being supported up to around 1800mm centres. Panels can be curved by setting them into a pre-formed aluminium edge frame, when the material can be curved to a minimum radius of 1500mm for twin wall sheets and around 4000mm for the thickest sheets.

Plastic-composite flat panels usually have a mixture of around 70 per cent softwood fibre and 30 per cent resin, manufactured at high temperature and pressure to provide coloured panels of smooth and almost impervious surface. Although the finish colour is formed by using pigmented resins as a top coat in the mould, the colour extends all the way through the material, allowing cut edges to be visible. Plastic-composite panels have high UV resistance, high colour stability, high fire resistance and can be cut and drilled easily, allowing them to be used as overlapping tiles in the manner of timber shingles. Their high impact resistance makes them well suited to conditions susceptible to damage. The material is made in sheet sizes from 3600mm × 1800mm, 3000mm × 1500mm and 2500mm × 1800mm in thicknesses from around 5mm to 12mm. Corner panels and parapets are also manufactured in the same material. Plastic-composite flat panels can be fixed with visible fixings or concealed point fixings.

Section 1:10. Ground level

The renewed interest in timber framed construction for both façades and complete building structures has led to the development of prefabricated modular designs such as the two examples illustrated here. The Artist's Studio in Utrecht by Korteknie Stuhlmacher is conceived as a mobile building, and has a corresponding sense of physical lightness. This building comprises visually distinct modules which can be separated for transportation and re-assembly. The idea of a partially unfolding box is expressed by walls that lower to become access decks. The Muster Haus by Oscar Leo Kaufmann uses modular boards as the external cladding material in a design that contrasts large areas of glazing with large uninterrupted areas of cladding, while remaining within the logic of timber framing. Rainscreen construction can be used to provide visual screens and moveable solar shading panels, as demonstrated in the Peninsular House by Sean Godsell. Successive layers of screens within the building provide a sense of depth which is mirrored in the timber decking.

06_
timber

Photographs. Top (left to right): Mobile Artist's Studio, Utrecht, Holland. Architect: Korteknie Stuhlmacher; Peninsular House, Victoria, Australia. Architect: Sean Godsell; Muster Haus, Germany. Architect: Oscar Leo Kaufmann.
Opposite page: Peninsular House, Victoria, Australia. Architect: Sean Godsell

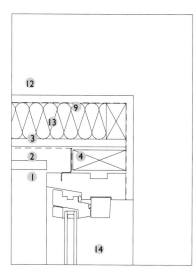

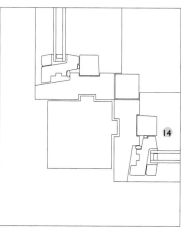

Section 1:10. Parapet

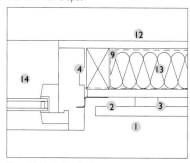

Plans 1:10. Window jambs

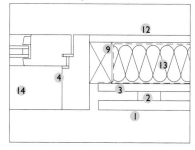

Design considerations

There are two enduring traditional generic forms of loadbearing timber frame that use small section timbers to form framed loadbearing walls: the platform frame and the balloon frame. Both the platform frame and the balloon frame are based on softwood sawn timber sections. The platform frame comprises studs spanning from floor to floor, with the timber floor structure being supported at each storey height set of timber frames. The balloon frame, which is now used to a much lesser extent, is enjoying a revival in light gauge steel sections. This method has vertical framing members which are continuous, with the intermediary floors being supported by the wall running continuously past it.

Timber frames comprise studs (vertical sections) fixed to rails (horizontal members) which are clad with plywood sheathing to provide lateral bracing, typically 12mm–18mm thick, depending on panel size and loads. Timber boards can also be used as sheathing, but this is a less economic solution. Framing members are typically formed from 100 x 50mm softwood sections at 400mm vertical centres which are nailed together. Voids between the framing members are filled with thermal insulation. A breather membrane is then fixed to the face of the sheathing layer. This provides a waterproof barrier which also allows the vapour to escape to allow the timber wall to release and absorb moisture with changes in the weather. Outer timber cladding boards are then fixed on the outside of the breather membrane.

Traditionally, timber cladding was used to stiffen the structural frame by fixing the boarding directly to the frame, with a breather membrane set between the frame and the timber boards as a weatherproof layer. More recently, the timber cladding is fixed to battens set forward of the breather membrane, or waterproofing layer, to ensure that the timber is ventilated on both sides. The inside face of the timber framed wall has a continuous vapour barrier set (in temperate climates) on the warm in winter side of the wall. The inner face of the wall is then finished with a dry lining.

Design solutions

Timber cladding at ground level stops a minimum of 150mm above external ground level. Cladding is usually supported at ground level on a concrete slab or edge beam that forms part of the concrete wall. Alternatively, the wall can span between concrete pads at 3000mm-5000mm centres, with timber beams at the base of the wall to provide support between pads. Where a concrete slab is used, the edge of the slab has traditionally been exposed as a base to the wall. Thermal insulation is set on the visible edge of the slab with an additional outer protection, typically a thin concrete panel or brick skin.

The timber wall frame is usually set on a continuous timber section at ground level, which is first fixed to the concrete slab to provide a level surface to set the timber in place. A damp proof course (DPC) is set beneath the continuous timber base plate usually extending down the vertical face of the concrete slab where it connects with the damp proof membrane (DPM) beneath the concrete slab or the vertical face of the basement wall. The DPC is also made continuous with the DPM set on top of the concrete slab. Where concrete foundation pads are used, the timber beam is set into stainless steel shoes fixed to the pads. Timber can also be supported on brick walls set at a minimum of 150mm above external ground level and be supported on a concrete strip foundation or ground beam. A raised floor is then set into this brick wall. The void beneath the timber floor is ventilated with air bricks that encourage cross ventilation. This avoids stagnant air in the void from damaging and eventually rotting the timber floor.

Corners, both external and internal type, are formed typically with a timber bead set so that the timber boards on both sides butt into it. If a breather membrane is used behind the cladding, then an additional waterproof flashing is added to the corner. This is formed in a durable polymer-based sheet or metal sheet. Alternatively, the boards can be allowed to make a corner with a butt joint, and an additional L-shaped timber trim, formed from two separate timber sections, is added on the face of the corner to protect the exposed end grain of one of the sides forming the corner. Boards can be joined with a mitred joint without any cover strip but the timber used must be of high quality to avoid the joint opening up with moisture movement. A waterproof layer or flashing is set behind the mitred joint.

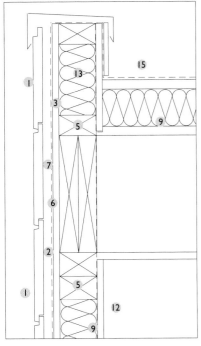

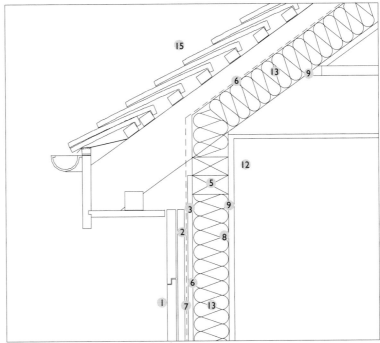

Section 1:10. Eaves conditions to pitched roof

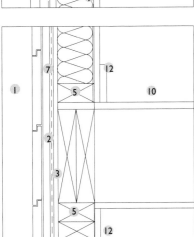

Details

1. Timber boards
2. Timber battens
3. Plywood sheathing
4. Timber studs
5. Timber rail
6. Breather membrane
7. Air cavity
8. Damp proof course/membrane
9. Vapour barrier
10. Timber floor
11. Concrete ground slab
12. Internal finish or dry lining
13. Thermal insulation quilt
14. Timber framed window
15. Roof construction

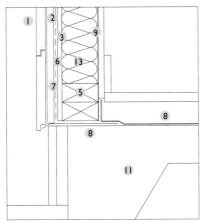

Section 1:10. Typical wall assembly

Muster Haus, Germany. Architect: Oscar Leo Kaufmann

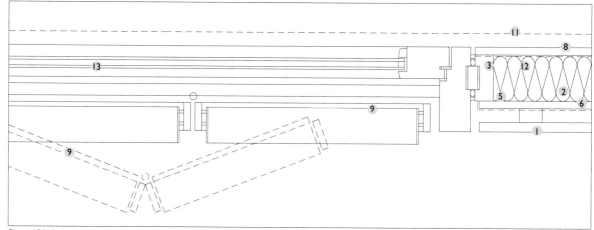

Plan 1:10. Window jambs

Details
1. Timber boards
2. Plywood sheathing
3. Timber stud
4. Timber rail
5. Breather membrane
6. Air cavity
7. Damp proof course
8. Vapour barrier
9. Solar shading screen
10. Concrete floor slab
11. Internal finish or dry lining
12. Thermal insulation quilt
13. Timber framed window
14. Timber cill
15. Additional metal trim shown

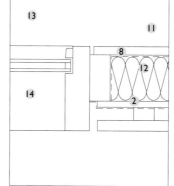
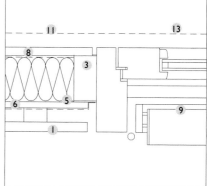

Plan 1:10. Typical cladding panel with additional solar shading or guarding.

Design considerations

Timber cladding panels are fixed to a structural frame typically in reinforced concrete, steel or timber. Because of the higher moisture movement associated with timber, junctions between cladding panels requires allowance for both structural movements and moisture movements in the frame within the timber.

Where timber cladding panels are set forward of the floor slabs in the manner of glazed curtain walling, panels span from floor to floor, either hung from a floor slab or, more typically, supported on it at floor level. Timber cladding is used increasingly as the inner wall in twin wall construction, where an outer glazed wall provides protection to allow the windows to be opened for natural ventilation as well as protecting the appearance of the timber by not exposing it to outside conditions. Vertical joints between panels have a stepped joint to allow for deflections in floor slabs between panels, following principles of

glazed curtain walling. This stepped joint is covered on the outside with timber boards, set forward of the face of panels on battens in rainscreen configuration. The construction of panels follows the same principle of timber cladding described in the previous section. Horizontal joints have an inner chamber formed between two adjacent panels. Any rainwater that penetrates the outer seal, which is also kept open in some designs, is drained down an inner chamber where the water is discharged through the horizontal joint at the bottom of the panel.

Where cladding panels are set onto floor slabs, and restrained at the slab above, timber posts forming part of the structure may also be set between panels rather than inside the building, since there is no significant thermal bridge from outside to inside, allowing the structural frame to be exposed on the outside. Cladding panels are set into openings in the laminated timber frame, with panels supported at their base on the tops of beams.

Floor decks in timber are then fixed to the side of the laminated timber beams. Timber panels are fixed at their base to the beam beneath, but have a sliding restraint at the top to allow the slab and panel above to deflect without damaging the panel below. A metal flashing at the base of the panel drains water and throws it clear of the beam beneath in order to avoid staining. The outer timber rainscreen cladding is set flush with the outer face of the laminated timber frame to avoid any views into the waterproofing layer behind.

Design solutions

Both softwoods and hardwoods are used for cladding panels, with durable hardwoods being more commonly used for rainscreen applications. Where less expensive, less durable timbers are used, higher levels of both finishing and maintenance are required. Softwood boards are made usually in 250mm widths, with trimmed boards with profiles routed into them usually trimmed down to 150-200mm widths. All timbers vary in moisture content with changes in temperature and air humidity, this being one of the essential aspects to be considered in timber detailing. Most timbers used in cladding will have a moisture content from around 5 per cent to 20 per cent when in use.

Timber cladding is finished with the timber being left either as supplied, with preservative applied or injected by the supplier, or alternatively is given coats of preservative in clear, stained, or opaque finish on site with preservatives that repel rainwater, or wood stains and paint. Paints can be oil-based or acrylic,

while preservatives are clear and can be used as a finish that does not appreciably change its appearance. It can also be used before staining or painting the timber. Preservatives help to prevent moisture absorption as well as reduce fungal growth. This is because they enhance the life of the timber but do not prevent the material changing colour and fading to a silver grey appearance.

The most common traditional types of jointing of boards is 'ship lapping' where timber boards are set horizontally and lapped over one another with the upper board lapped over the top of the board below to protect it from rainwater ingress. Ship lap-

ping can be assisted by the use of 'feathered' or wedge-shaped boards to give the lapping a more elegant appearance. Tongue-and-groove boards are used to give a continuous flat appearance, while having the advantage of locking boards together into a continuous layer. Boards are typically around 20mm thick, made in lengths around 3000mm-3500mm, to avoid vertical joints which are a potential source of rainwater penetration except in rainscreen configuration.

Peninsular House, Victoria, Australia. Architect: Sean Godsell

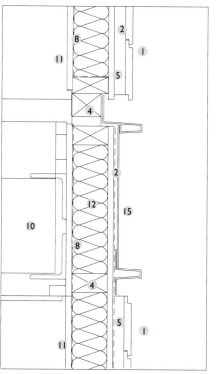

Elevation 1:10. Typical build-up of cladding panel

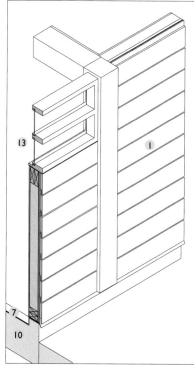

Isometric views of wall assembly

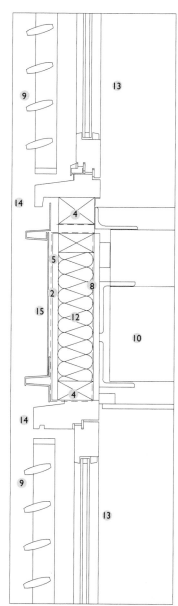

Section 1:10. Junction with floor slab

This bibliography lists articles from the international technical press from the years 1990 to 2005. The subject matter of these articles covers general issues about the nature and the future of façade construction, from a materials-based standpoint.

AA FILES
no. 31, Summer 1996.
'Truth to material' vs 'the principle of cladding': the language of materials in architecture.

A+T
no. 14, 1999.
Special issue. Materiales sensibles [Sensitive materials].

ARCA
no. 129, September 1998.
Special issue. Superfici [Surfaces].

ARCHITECT (THE HAGUE)
vol. 30, no. 5, May 1999.
Grotere rijkheid met eenvoudiger middelen. Vlies – en metselwekgevels van Rudy Uytenhaak [Greater richness with a choice of materials. Prefabrication and preshaping of materials are the primary methods used].

ARQUITECTURA VIVA
no. 54, May/June 1997.
Berlin de piedra. Revestimientos de fachada: ?variedad en la unidad? [Berlin in stone. Recladding façades: variety in unity?]

ARCHITECTURE NEW ZEALAND
May/June, 1999.
Skin game.

ARCHITECTURE INTERIEURE CREE
no. 289, 1999.
Special issue. Friches / renovation / reconversion [Renovation and conversion of disused buildings].

ARCHITECTURE MOUVEMENT CONTINUITE
no. 20, April 1988.
Façades industrielles [Industrial façades].

ARCHITECTURE TODAY
no. 98, May 1999.
Innovation: a vision of the construction industry twenty years from now predicts far-reaching changes.

ARCHITECTURAL RECORD
October 1995.
The Intelligent Exterior.

ARCHITECTURAL REVIEW
vol. 194, no. 1167, May 1994.
Special issue. Materiality.

ARCHITECTURAL REVIEW
January 1995.
Light spirited.

ARCHITECTURAL REVIEW
vol. 202, no. 1208, October 1997.
Special issue. Nature of materials.

ARCHITECTURAL REVIEW
vol. 207, no. 1239, May 2000.
Special issue. Materiality.

ARCHITECTURAL REVIEW
May 2002.
Material witnesses.

ARCHITECTURAL REVIEW
February 2003.
The New Paradigm in Architecture.

ARCHITECTURAL REVIEW
June 2003.
The search for climate responsive architecture.

ARCHITEKT
no. 1, January 1997.
Okologische Bewertung von Baustoffen [The ecological assessment of construction materials].

ARCHITEKT
no. 5, May 1998.
Special issue. Fassade – Gesicht, Haut oder Hulle? [A façade – the face, the skin or the cladding?]

ARCHITEKT
no. 11, November 1999.
Special issue. Im Reich der Erfindung [In the realm of invention].

ARCHITEKT
no. 3, March 2000.
Planung und Ausfuhrung: Glasfassaden [Design and implementation: glass façades].

ARCHITEKTUR (BERLIN)
vol. 40, no. 8, August 1991.
Vorgehangte Fassaden [Façades].

ARCHITHESE
vol. 22, no. 3, May/June 1992.
Special issue. Nur Fassade [Façades].

BAUMEISTER
vol. 93, no. 8, August 1996.
Neue Baustoffe [New materials].

BAUMEISTER
vol. 95, no. 7, July 1998.
Special issue. Neue Oberflachen – Material als architektonisches Programm [New surfaces – materials as architectural programme].

BAUWELT
vol. 87, no. 16, April 26, 1996.
Aufs Ganze gehen Glasfassaden [Go all the way with glass façades].

BAUWELT
vol. 87, no. 43/44, November 22, 1996.
Auf dem Prufstand [From the test bed].

BAUWELT
vol. 88, no. 7, February 1997.
Naturstein [Natural stone].

BAUWELT
vol. 91, no. 3, January 21, 2000.
Von den Materialien [On materials].

CASABELLA
June 1996.
Le pareti ventilate [Ventilated walls].

DETAIL
vol. 30, no. 4, August/September 1990.
Special issue. Fassaden-Konstruktionen [Façade systems].

DETAIL
vol. 33, no. 3, June/July 1993.
Special issue. Metallfassaden [Metal façade constructions].

DETAIL
vol. 36, no. 4, June 1996.
Special issue. Fassade, Fenster [Façades and fenestration].

DETAIL
vol. 38, no. 1, January/February 1998.
Special issue. Einfaches Bauen [Simple forms of building].

DETAIL
vol. 38, no. 7, October/November 1998.
Special issue. Fassaden [Façades].

DETAIL
July 2001.
Façades

DETAIL
July/August 2003.
Façades/Envelopes.

DEUTSCHE BAUZEITSCHRIFT
vol. 38, no. 4, April 1990.
Fassaden mit Stahlbauteilen [Façades
with steel elements].

DEUTSCHE BAUZEITSCHRIFT
vol. 40, no. 8, August 1992.
Die Dreidimensionalitat der Fassaden-
Verschraubung [The three
dimensionality of screwing together
façades].

DEUTSCHE BAUZEITSCHRIFT
vol. 45, no. 5, May 1997.
Auswahl von Baumaterialien.
Gegenwartige trends und zukunftiges
Potential [Choice of building materials.
Contemporary trends and future
potential].

DEUTSCHE BAUZEITUNG
vol. 130, no. 1, January 1996.
Materialien [Materials].

DEUTSCHE BAUZEITUNG
vol. 131, no. 10, October 1997.
Chemie im Schafspelz? Dammstoffe aus
Altpapier oder Naturfasern – (k)eine
Alternative? [Insulating material from old
paper or natural fibre – an alternative/no
alternative?]

DEUTSCHE BAUZEITUNG
vol. 133, no. 8, August 1999.
Fluch und Segen [PVC recycling in
building materials].

DOMUS
no. 756, January 1994.
Materiali e progetto [Materials and
design].

DOMUS
no. 789, January 1997.
Leapfrog – progettare la sostenibilita
[Leapfrog – designing sustainability].

DOMUS
no. 801, February 1998.
Materialita [Materiality].

DOMUS
no. 818, September 1999.
Special issue. Impara dalla natura
[Learning from nature].

ECO
vol. 38, no. 7, October/November 1998.
For green, try blue.

ECO DESIGN
vol. 6, no. 2, 1998.
Special issue. Eco design around the
world.

GLASFORUM
vol. 39, no. 3, June 1989.
Tendenzen der Glasarchitektur:
Glasfassadenkonzepte aus England
[Trends in glass architecture: glass
façades from England].

MONITEUR ARCHITECTURE AMC
no. 22, June 1991.
Details: les façades metalliques [Details:
metal façades].

MONITEUR ARCHITECTURE AMC
no. 70, April 1996.
Façades: les bardages metalliques
[Façades: metal cladding].

MONITEUR ARCHITECTURE AMC
no. 75, November 1996.
Façade: panneaux de bois [Façades:
timber panels].

MONITEUR ARCHITECTURE AMC
no. 83, October 1997.
Les façades.

PROGRESSIVE ARCHITECTURE,
February 1994.
What makes a good curtain wall?

PROGRESSIVE ARCHITECTURE
March 1994.
The ends of finishing.

PROGRESSIVE ARCHITECTURE
June 1994.
Amazing glazing.

QUADERNS
No. 202, 1994.
La flexibilidad come dispositivo
[Flexibility as a device].

RECUPERARE
vol. 10, no. 9, November/December
1991.
La valutazione delle facciate ventilate
[The evaluation of ventilated façades].

RECUPERARE EDILIZIA DESIGN
IMPIANTI
vol. 2, no. 8, November/December 1983.
Ventilated façades in building
rehabilitation.

SOLAR ENERGY
June 1996.
Numerical study of a ventilated façade
panel.

TECHNIQUES & ARCHITECTURE
December-January 1994.
Façade Legere et menuiserie metallique
[Lightweight façades and metal joinery].

TECHNIQUES & ARCHITECTURE
no. 413, April/May 1994.
La dimension ecologique [The ecological
dimension].

TECHNIQUES & ARCHITECTURE
no. 422, October/November 1995.
Revetements de façade [Covering
façades].

TECHNIQUES & ARCHITECTURE
no. 430, February/March 1997.
Beton en parement [Concrete as
adornment].

TECHNIQUES & ARCHITECTURE
no. 448, April/May 2000.
De la matiere [Material matters].

TECHNIQUES & ARCHITECTURE
October 2002.
Matériaux innovants et applications à
l'usage des architectes. [Innovative
materials and applications for the use of
architects].

TECHNIQUES & ARCHITECTURE
June-July 2003.
Matériaux imprimés, gravés, sculptés,
sérigraphiés en façade. [Printed
materials, etched sculpted aand screen
printed on façades].

Most commonly used British Standards for façades

BS EN ISO 140-3. Acoustics. Measurement of sound insulation in buildings and of building elements – Part 3: Laboratory measurement of airborne sound insulation of building elements.

BS EN 410. Glass in building. Determination of luminous and solar characteristics of glazing.

BS EN ISO 717-1. Acoustics. Rating of sound insulation in buildings and of building elements – Part 1: Airborne sound insulation.

BS EN 795. Protection against falls from a height. Anchor devices. Requirements and testing.

BS 874-3. Methods for determining thermal insulating properties – Part 3: Tests for thermal transmittance and conductance.

BS EN 1026. Windows and doors. Air permeability. Test method.

BS EN 1027. Windows and doors. Watertightness. Test method.

DD ENV 1627. Windows, doors, shutters. Burglar resistance. Requirements and classification.

BS EN 1808. Safety requirements on suspended access equipment. Design calculations, stability criteria, construction. Tests.

BS 5080-1. Structural fixings in concrete and masonry – Part 1: Method of test for tensile loading.

BS 5080-2. Structural fixings in concrete and masonry – Part 2: Method for determination of resistance to loading in shear.

BS 5250. Code of practice for control of condensation in buildings.

BS 5516-1. Patent glazing and sloping glazing for buildings – Part 1: Code of practice for design and installation of sloping and vertical patent glazing.

BS 5516-2. Patent glazing and sloping glazing for buildings – Part 2: Code of practice for sloping glazing.

BS 5534. Code of practice for slating and tiling (including shingles).

BS 6229. Code of practice for flat roofs with continuously supported coverings.

BS 6262-5. Glazing for buildings – Part 5: Code of practice for frame design considerations.

BS 6375-1. Performance of windows – Part 1: Classification for weathertightness and guidance on selection and specification.

BS 6375-2. Performance of windows - Part 2: Specification for operation and strength characteristics.

BS 6399-1. Loading for buildings – Part 1: Code of practice for dead and imposed loads.

BS 6399-2. Loading for buildings – Part 2: Code of practice for wind loads.

BS 6399-3. Loading for buildings – Part 3: Code of practice for imposed roof loads.

PD 6484. Commentary on corrosion at bimetallic contacts and its alleviation.

BS 6651. Code of practice for protection of structures against lightning.

BS 7543. Guide to durability of buildings and building elements, products and components.

BS 7671. Requirements for electrical installations. IEE Wiring Regulations. Sixteenth edition.

BS 7883. Code of practice for the design, selection installation, use and maintenance of anchor devices conforming to BS EN 795.

ES 7950. Specification for enhanced security performance of casement and tilt/turn windows for domestic applications.

BS 7985. Code of Practice for the use of rope access methods for industrial purposes.

BS 8000-7. Workmanship on building sites – Part 7: Code of practice for glazing.

BS 8118-1. Structural use of aluminium – Part 1: Code of practice for design.

BS 8118-2. Structural use of aluminium – Part 2: Specification for materials, workmanship and protection.

BS 8200. Code of practice for design of non-loadbearing external vertical enclosures of buildings.

BS 8213-1. Windows, doors and rooflights – Part 1: Design for safety in use and during cleaning of windows, including door-height windows and roof windows. Code of practice.

BS 8297. Code of practice for Design and installation of non-loadbearing precast concrete cladding.

BS 8300. Design of buildings and their approaches to meet the needs of disabled people – Code of practice.

BS 8437. Code of practice for selection, use and maintenance of personal fall protection systems and equipment for use in the workplace.

BS EN 12152. Curtain walling – Air permeability – Performance requirements and classification.

BS EN 12153. Curtain walling – Air permeability – Test method.

BS EN 12154. Curtain walling – Watertightness – Performance requirements and classification.

BS EN 12155. Curtain walling – Watertightness – Laboratory test under static pressure.

BS EN 12179. Curtain walling – Resistance to wind load – Test method.

BS EN 12400. Windows and pedestrian doors. Mechanical durability. Requirements and classification.

BS EN 12600. Glass in building. Pendulum test. Impact test method and classification for flat glass.

BS EN 13116. Curtain walling – Resistance to wind load – Performance requirements.

BS EN 13022-1*. Glass in building. Structural sealant glazing – Part 1: Actions, requirements and terminology.

BS EN 13022-2*. Glass in building. Structural sealant glazing – Part 2: Product standard for ultra violet resistant sealant and structural sealant.

BS EN 13022-3*. Glass in building. Structural sealant glazing – Part 3: Sealants. Test methods.

BS EN 13022-4*. Glass in building. Structural sealant glazing – Part 4: Assembly rules.

BS EN 13030. Ventilation for buildings. Terminals. Performance testing of louvres subjected to simulated rain.

DD ENV 13050. Curtain walling – Watertightness – laboratory test under dynamic condition of air pressure and water spray.

BS EN 13051. Curtain walling – Watertightness – Site test.

BS EN 13501-1. Fire classification of construction products and building elements – Part 1: Classification using test data from reaction to fire tests.

BS EN 13501-2. Fire classification of construction products and building elements – Part 2: Classification using data from fire resistance tests, excluding ventilation services.

BS EN ISO 13788. Hygrothermal performance of building components and building elements. Internal surface temperature to avoid critical surface humidity and interstitial condensation. Calculation methods.

BS EN 13830. Curtain walling product standard.

BS EN 14019. Curtain walling. Impact resistance. Performance requirements.

ISO 15099. Thermal performance of windows, doors and shading devices – Detailed calculations.

BS EN 15686-1. Buildings and constructed assets – Service life planning – Part 1: General principles.

BS EN 15686-2. Buildings and constructed assets – Service life planning – Part 2: Service life prediction procedures.

BS EN ISO 15927. Hygrothermal performance of buildings. Calculation and presentation of climatic data – Part 1: Monthly means of single meteorological elements.

* Standards under development.

Associated documents

ACPO. Secured by design
http://www.securedbydesign.com

ACR(M)001. Test for non-fragility of profiled sheeted roofing assemblies, http://www. roofworkadvice.info

BRE. Avoiding summertime solar overheating.

BRE Digest 228. Estimation of thermal and moisture movements and stresses – Part 2.

BRE Digest 229. Estimation of thermal and moisture movements and stresses – Part 3.

BRE Digest 301. Corrosion of metals by wood.

BRE Digest 346-7. The assessment of wind loads – Part 7: Wind speeds for serviceability and fatigue.

CFA. Procedure for site testing construction fixings, Construction Fixings Association, htpp://www.fixingscfa.co.uk

CWCT. Guide to the selection and testing of stone panels for external use.

CWCT. The thermal assessment of window assemblies, curtain walling and non-traditional walls.

CWCT. Design of façades for safety: access for construction, maintenance and repair.

CWCT. Standard for specifying and assessing condensation risk.

CWCT TN 33. Breather membranes and vapour control layers in walls.

CWCT TN 38. Acoustic performance of windows.

CWCT TN 39. Sound transmission through building envelopes.
CWCT TN 41. Site testing for watertightness.

CWCT TN 42. Safety and fragility of glazed roofing.

CWCT TN 52. Impact performance of cladding.

CWCT TN 53. Method statements for the construction of building envelopes.

DDA. Disability Discrimination Act 1995.

ETAG 001 Guideline for European Technical Approval for metal anchors for use in concrete.

ETAG 002 Guideline for European Technical Approval for structural sealant glazing systems.

HMSO. Construction Design and Management Regulations Statutory Instrument 1994 No 3140, http://www.opsi.gov.uk.

HMSO. Work at Height Regulations Statutory Instrument 2005 No 735, http://www.opsi.gov.uk.

LPS 1175. Burglary Resistant Building Components, Strongpoints and Security Enclosures, Loss Prevention Certification Board.

MOAT 7. Internal and external doorsets.

MOAT 22. UEAtc Directives for the assessment of external insulation systems for walls (expanded polystyrene insulation faced with a thin rendering), British Board of Agrément.

PAS 24-1. Enhanced security performance requirements for door assemblies – Part 1: Single leaf, external door assemblies to dwellings.

PD 6484. Commentary on corrosion at bi-metallic contacts and alleviation.

TRADA. External timber cladding, Patrick Hislop, 2000.

TRADA 2/3-33. TRADA Wood information sheet 2/3-33, http://www.trada.co.uk